LIVING FAITHFULLY

as a Prayer Book People

LIVING FAITHFULLY

as a Prayer Book People

JOHN H. WESTERHOFF

morehouse

HARRISBURG • LONDON

Copyright © 2004 by John H. Westerhoff

Morehouse Publishing, P.O. Box 1321, Harrisburg, PA 17105

Morehouse Publishing, The Tower Building, 11 York Road, London SE1 7NX

Morehouse Publishing is a Continuum imprint.

Unless otherwise noted, Scripture quotations contained herein are from the New Revised Standard Version Bible, copyright © 1989 by the Division of Christian Education of the National Council of the Churches of Christ in the U.S.A. Used by permission. All rights reserved.

Cover design: Laurie Klein Westhafer

Library of Congress Cataloging-in-Publication Data

Westerhoff, John H.
  Living faithfully as a prayer book people / by John H. Westerhoff.
    p. cm.
  ISBN 0-8192-1950-9 (pbk.)
  1. Episcopal Church. Book of common prayer (1979) 2. Episcopal Church—Liturgy. 3. Anglican Communion—Liturgy. 4. Christian life—Anglican authors.
I. Title.
  BX5945.W47 2005
  264'.03—dc22

                              2004018146

Printed in the United States of America

04 05 06 07 08 09   10 9 8 7 6 5 4 3 2 1

Dedicated with love to my wife Caroline

CONTENTS

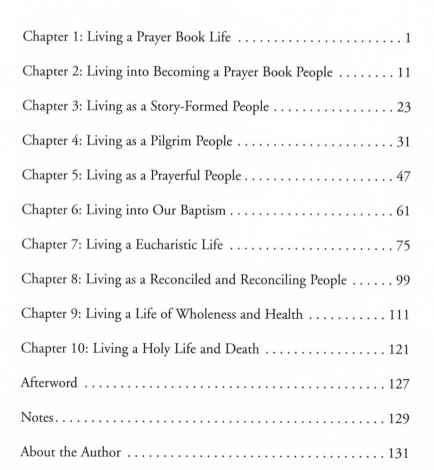

CHAPTER 1
LIVING A PRAYER BOOK LIFE

It is not easy to define an Episcopalian.[1] Yet, in spite of all our differences, we have one outstanding characteristic: We are a prayer book people.

The Anglican Communion represents the continuous tradition of the one, holy, catholic, and apostolic church in England, which became a distinctive entity, the Church of England, during the Reformation era. The Anglican Communion is one of the four divisions of Christianity, the others being the Eastern Orthodox churches, the Roman Catholic Church, and the Protestant churches. The Anglican Communion is comprised of thirty-eight separate national churches or provinces that recognize each other as members of a common tradition within Christianity. A few of these are the Anglican Church of Canada, the Anglican Church of Australia, the Episcopal Church in the United States, the Episcopal Church in Scotland, and the Anglican Church of South Africa. While each province is autonomous and self-governing, they are bound together as a spiritual family in which the community of bishops is intended to play a unifying role.

Fundamentally, Anglicans (that includes us Episcopalians) are Christians who worship according to some authorized edition of a Book of Common Prayer and are in communion with the See of Canterbury in England. Our primary identity is as a community of practice. That is, we are bound together by our liturgy rather than by doctrinal propositions, moral absolutes, or social organization. Orthodoxy for us is right worship more than right belief. Our life of prayer shapes our beliefs, attitudes, and behaviors. To answer what we believe about the Christian life of faith, we turn to our prayer book and engage in a process of interpreting its content.

For us, theological and ethical issues typically become issues concerning our liturgies. We shape our understanding of faith and life through participation in our liturgies. We reflect on our convictions about faith and life by reflecting on our liturgies. We reform our understandings and ways of life by revising our liturgies

It is, therefore, incumbent upon us to explore our identity by reflecting on what it means to be a prayer book people, a tradition in which our understanding of liturgical life encompasses both our ritual life of communal public worship and our daily lives and work as ministry. If others are to understand who we are, indeed, if we are to understand ourselves, we need to participate in our prayer book liturgies and minister together; that is, to serve God every day, in every moment, and in every place we find ourselves.

The purpose of this book is to take a journey through the Book of Common Prayer 1979. We will reflect on its content and comment on its connections with our daily lives.

Human Nature

To begin, to be a prayer book people is to acknowledge that we humans are relational beings, communal persons. As Pascal put it, "One Christian is no Christian." We cannot be Christian outside the church, outside a community of faith and its worship and ministry. There are those who contend that they are spiritual, but not religious. From a Christian perspective, I contend that this is not possible. Christianity is an incarnational, embodied faith. The spiritual life and institutional religion cannot be separated from each other. Another way to say it is this: Personal religion and public worship are interdependent. The drama of the church's history lies in the tensions between these two dimensions and their rival claims.

In her book *Worship,* Evelyn Underhill[2] explains that the worship life of a Christian, while profoundly personal, is essentially that of a person who is a member of a community. Our personal relationship with God is maintained and kept healthy insofar as we regularly participate in communal worship.

Willard Sperry, Bartlet Professor of Sacred Rhetoric and dean of the Divinity School in Harvard University in 1925, wrote in *Reality in Worship:*

> Wherever and whenever men meet together avowedly to address themselves to the act of worship, there is the church, clearly and distinctly defined. . . . If the church does nothing else for the world other than keep open a house, symbolic of the homeland of the human soul, where in season and out of season men reaffirm their faith in the universal fatherhood of God, it is doing the social order the greatest possible service and no other service which it renders society can compare in importance to this. . . . So long as the church bids men to the worship of God and provides a simple and credible vehicle for worship it need not question its place, mission, and influence in the world. If it loses faith in the act of worship, is thoughtless in the ordering of worship, and careless in the conduct of worship, it need not look to its avocations to save it. It is dead at its heart."[3]

Cultic Life and Daily Life

The word *liturgy* in Greek means public service, and this public service has two dimensions: communal worship or cultic life and daily life and work. Cultic life, which encompasses the world of symbols, myths, and rituals, influences a community's life and work in the world. And how we live, personally and communally, is both a consequence and a test of our cultic faithfulness. Another way to say it is that our habitual participation in a community's cultic life—in those repetitive symbolic acts (word and deed) that express and manifest a community's sacred narratives or myths—shapes our faith or perceptions of life; shapes our characters or our identity and how we are disposed to act; and shapes our consciousness or the subjective awareness that makes particular experiences, like the presence of God, possible. For this reason, throughout history, when the church concluded that it was not living as faithfully as it should, it reformed its rituals. And in general, many people were uncomfortable with these changes because they knew at least unconsciously that if they were to change their ritual life it would influence them to change their daily lives.

To communicate this eternal truth, when Leonard Bernstein was commissioned to compose a piece of music for the opening of the Kennedy Center in Washington, D.C., he set the text of the Latin mass to music with one important difference. Each Latin text is followed by a folk song in English, revealing the dissonance between, on the one hand, what we say and do in our rituals and, on the other, how we conduct our daily lives.

Thus "Confiteor" (I confess) is followed by a song: "What I say I don't feel, what I feel I don't show." The function of the English text is to expose our blithe "confiteors" to enable each of us to make a more honest confession. But Bernstein did not stop there. He knew that all ritual, in this case the ritual of the Eucharist, belongs to a community, not simply to a collection of individuals.

As Bernstein's *Mass* begins, a young man in blue jeans gathers people around him and dons the vestments of celebration. By all appearances, these people are a Christian community. But Bernstein aptly paraphrases an axiom from Paul's first letter to the Christian community in Corinth, "Because we eat one bread, we are not necessarily one at all."

Christian unity and community are not solely the result of hymns sung in unison or magnificent anthems sung by choirs. As the *Mass* proceeds, we see that there are only private meanings in what this group of worshippers do together. They prefer ceremonies that support their private perceptions and lives to the challenging mystery of God's reconciling presence. They prefer music and drama well performed to commitments of faith.

Bernstein then proceeds to illustrate his point. When the piece was produced at Duke University where I once taught, it manifested itself in a particularly dramatic form. The director attempted to show Bernstein, the Jew, trying to make sense of the potentially universal split between cultic and daily life for *all* religions. The altar was placed on a mountaintop and the celebrant stood above the congregation holding the symbols of Christ's presence, consecrated bread and wine, just as Moses had done with the tablets on Mount Sinai. But we did not see the Israelites carousing about as they did in the golden calf episode—no, these folk were playing at institutional church. And just as Moses hurled the commandments to the ground, the priest hurled down the symbols of Christ's presence and sang, "Things get broken so easily." A prophetic word in the midst of this sacred meal.

There are many reasons for the split between cultic life and daily life. Let's consider a few. First, we live with and participate in many conflicting rituals, such as spectator sports and television advertising, which also aim to influence how we perceive life and our lives as well as how we are to live. Second, our rituals may be inadequate; that is, they lack the character of good ritual. For example, if our rituals focus solely on intellectual or intuitive ways of thinking and knowing, to the neglect of the other, they are inadequate. Third, our rituals may be ineffective because the symbolic action they invite us to participate in may not point to and embrace the moral behaviors we desire. For example, they may encourage us to be individual observers rather than communal participants, or they may encourage us to live a passive rather than an active life. And fourth, our rituals can support and encourage unhealthy ways of life; that is, they can support escape rather than engagement, comfort rather than transformation, and so forth.[4]

The Dynamics of Religion

To provide us with a mechanism for connecting our cultic and daily lives, English sociologist Bruce Reed, in his book *The Dynamics of Religion*,[5] describes life as a process of oscillation in which people move back and forth from the structured, rational world of daily life and work to the anti-structured, intuitive world of cultic life. The church encourages this movement as a movement between two types of healthy dependence. Cultic life properly focuses our dependent needs for meaning and purpose on God. Reed calls this parent-child relationship "extra-dependence." He contends that this totally dependent relation with God is necessary if we are to live meaningful, purposeful, healthy lives in intra-dependent, adult-adult relationships.

The weekly cycle of healthy human beings, he suggests, looks like this: We disengage from our daily life and work and regress into conscious extra-dependence on God, who nurtures us to reengage with the world of daily life and work and live in healthy relationships with others.

Perhaps a natural human experience will help us understand this process. Picture a parent and a young child in a park. The child is sitting on the parent's lap. Feeling secure, the child ventures forth to play. After being confronted by another child, falling off a swing, and the like, the child runs back and jumps into the parent's lap. After a period of nurture and nourishment, the child runs off and returns to the playground.

However, if the church's ritual life denies or neglects these extra-dependent needs for God and encourages people to seek the satisfaction of these needs in human experiences at worship or in other communal activities, it no longer serves a healthy purpose. Human life is not so much a series of linear events leading toward some goal as it is living between two alternating modes of experience, each having its own value. Our ability to deal with the demands of daily life is related to our willingness to turn to God—on whom we depend as we move from attempts to manage and master our environment to a healthier, resourceless helplessness, from attempts at ego control to a willingness to let go.

If the church does not provide an opportunity, especially through its cultic life, for its members to regress into a transforming experience of being lovingly embraced in the arms of a transcendent God, followed by the experience of being encouraged to move out into the world to live with others in communal relationships that witness to an immanent God's presence and action, the church has neglected its purpose.

Our weekly Eucharist is the means by which we fully realize the identity given to us at our baptism when we were incorporated into Christ's body, infused with Christ's character, and empowered to be Christ's presence in the world. When the body of Christ assembles, it is not primarily to praise God. It is to transform the lives of those who have assembled to be a more faithful body in the world. The Eucharist is a prelude to a weekly missionary sendoff. Nourished by eucharistic food, motivated by the witness to Christ's reconciling action, and inspired by the Holy Spirit, the church is equipped to engage in Christ's mission of reconciliation in the world.

We believe that human beings are created in the image of God and can, therefore, only be whole when united with God. Our common human vocation is to grow in an ever deepening and loving relationship with God. Or as St. Augustine put it, "O God, thou hast made us for thyself, and our hearts are restless until they find rest in thee." Prayer is anything we do that enhances and enlivens our relationship with God. We humans build churches, go to church, and share in formal acts of worship because this divine discontent stirs us and will not let us be.

It is through baptism that we are incorporated into Christ's body, the church, and it is baptism that makes us one and unites us. It is through our participation in the Eucharist that we affirm, support, nurture, and nourish this unity. A community that prays together stays together, no matter how differently each individual may interpret scripture or hold to particular doctrinal or moral convictions.

Churches, like families, can be functional or dysfunctional. They are functional when they encourage and enable people to acknowledge, accept, and confront the chaos of life and their inability to control it. They are healthy when they provide rituals that engage the imagination to bring participants into a relationship with God—who can transform chaos into meaning, despair into hope, torment into peace, sorrow into joy, brokenness into wholeness, sickness into health, death into life. And then, of course, healthy churches send their members forth armed with new vision and power.

Dysfunctional churches encourage regressions into withdrawal or denial and provide a fantasy world of escape. Their rituals fail to have a prophetic edge or don't lead to a confrontation with a living God. Instead, they attempt to provide an escape from reality through inspirational entertainment. Ritual can become so human and clergy centered that it can ignore God, or it can so focus on God that it doesn't confront us with human reality.

Healthy rituals enable us to face the human predicament, bring us in touch with the realities of life, and prepare us to become involved in the affairs of the world. The supportive aspects of community life, small groups, and multitudes of activities can prevent the oscillation process from functioning and turn people in on themselves. The test of our rituals is found in their ability to take both modes of life seriously and to aid people in moving from one to the other.

Symbols, Myths, and Rituals

While signs are objects with defined meanings, symbols point beyond themselves and have power in that they embody that to which they point. Myths are symbolic narratives. Rituals are repetitive symbolic actions (words and deeds) that express and manifest a community's symbolic narratives. They define the nature of goodness, truth, and beauty and provide life with meaning and purpose. Symbols, myths, and rituals encompass the intuitive way of thinking and knowing and are best expressed through the arts: dance, music, drama, poetry, painting, and sculpture, for example. Public worship is comprised of symbols, myths, and rituals and is intended to engage the imagination more than reason, the intellectual way of thinking and knowing. Religion is an art before it is a science. Public worship comes before theology. We Episcopalians are convinced that the life of prayer shapes the life of believing.

In *Theopoetic: Theology and the Religious Imagination,*[6] New Testament scholar and poet Amos Wilder makes a plea for the church to take more seriously the role of symbols and the pre-rational in the way we deal with experience. He points out that human nature and human societies are more deeply motivated by images and fabulations than by ideas.

Nevertheless, there is both an objective and a subjective dimension to our public worship. The history of worship is in part a history of the oscillation between one extreme and the other. Objective worship images God as transcendent mystery; it is worship addressed to God in which sacramental communion is central. In objective worship we experience the soul aspiring to God. Subjective worship images God as immanent friend; it is worship addressed to the worshipper in which the proclamation of the Word is central. In subjective worship we experience God tabernacling with us. Episcopal worship has striven to unite and emphasize both dimensions.

A Christian view of life looks for meaning in immanent, everyday reality by looking beyond what is given to a more all-encompassing transcendent reality. Through ritual, our souls (bodies, minds, and spirits) are engulfed and transported into another mode of reality. In ritual, the world as lived and the world as imagined fuse, thereby providing the possibility of a transformed sense of reality. So it is that, out of the context of ritual life, the Christian life of faith emerges. Our rituals are at the center of our human life and essential to keeping human life human. Because this is so, our rituals can also keep human life from being fully human. For this reason, the church as an intentional, ritual-centered community needs to continually reflect on its ritual life and, when necessary, reform it. The history of liturgical change through the reform of our Book of Common Prayer is a testimony to this truth.

Through the years, in our ever-constant quest to be faithful, we have revised our Book of Common Prayer and reformed our public worship. This has often been painful and difficult, because our liturgy is at the heart of our identity as Episcopalians and is the foundation of our theological and ethical convictions. To understand what it means to be an Episcopalian, therefore, we will need to explore how we became a prayer book people.

CHAPTER 2
LIVING INTO BECOMING A PRAYER BOOK PEOPLE

Insofar as the Book of Common Prayer is foundational to our identity and common life, it will be helpful if we have some understanding of how it has developed and matured over time, knowing that it must continue to evolve and change.

Our Episcopal/Anglican understanding of being a prayer book people developed over time. As such, it is the story of our continuing struggles to maintain unity amid diversity, to be fully catholic and fully Protestant, and to be grounded in a historic past and yet relevant to an ever-changing present context.

To begin, the history of the Christian church in the West can be divided into eras: the Apostolic Age from the first to fourth centuries; the Age of Christendom from the fourth to the tenth/eleventh centuries; the Age of Faith or the Middle Ages from the tenth/eleventh to the sixteenth; the Age of Reason or Modernity from the sixteenth to the twentieth/twenty-first; and a postmodern period, yet to be named, from the twentieth/twenty-first onward.

In the West, the tenth/eleventh centuries ushered in the Middle Ages and witnessed a split between the Christian East and West, as well as a rise in the power of the papacy and the gradual dominance of the Western church centered in Rome. While some differences in liturgical piety continued, a medieval synthesis in liturgical practice began to surface. While a variety of liturgical texts guided liturgical performance, the liturgy as the work of the people became solely the work of the clergy.

The end of this medieval synthesis and the birth of the Reformation in the sixteenth century were marked by numerous liturgical movements and their countermovements.

The history of our Book of Common Prayer tells the story of our continuing attempt to think theologically, using reason to connect scripture and tradition with culture, changing human experience, and new knowledge. As such, our prayer book is a testament to the way we reflect theologically.

Beginnings

During the sixteenth century in England, Henry VIII was king and Thomas Cranmer was the Archbishop of Canterbury. Henry was a staunch Roman Catholic and a critic of the emerging reform movement on the Continent. While Cranmer had been somewhat influenced by the Lutheran movement in Germany, he remained a loyal Roman Catholic. But Henry, the English parliament, Cranmer, and the Church in England had serious political differences with the Bishop of Rome over the English doctrine of the "divine right of kings," that is, the relationship between church and state. By an act of Parliament, it was established that the English sovereign would replace the Bishop of Rome as the head of the Church of England. But little changed in the church: The "reformation" in England had not yet begun. Doctrine and worship in what was now the Church of England continued as before, although there was some interest in translating the Mass and the scriptures into English, along with some other desires for reform.

On the Continent, however, there were tremendous changes taking place. The medieval synthesis had broken apart and a dramatic reformation had begun. The Age of Faith was about to become the Age of Reason. And no one could yet imagine how the Enlightenment might influence the church and its worship. While he was conservative in terms of liturgical change, Luther insisted that the scriptures should play a more central role in the liturgy and that both the scriptures and the church's rites be translated into German so that the people could fully participate. Calvin's theology and his understanding of worship went much further afield, and radical reformers like Zwingli went even further. All these various voices and their liturgical implications began to be taken seriously by different English clergy and scholars.

While Henry VIII remained the champion of Roman Catholic orthodoxy, he had, for unknown reasons, arranged for his son Edward to be educated by Protestant Calvinists, and he had made the Duke of Somerset, a committed reformer, the titular leader of the regency council that was to rule on his son's behalf until he came of age. Therefore, as soon as Henry VIII died and Edward VI become king, the reformation on the Continent finally reached England.

Cranmer continued as the Archbishop of Canterbury and was open to liturgical reform. He wanted to see a return to antiquity, greater simplicity, the liturgy in the language of the people, greater congregational participation (especially the administration of the Holy Communion to the laity in both kinds), and greater edification through the reading of scripture and preaching. He had already begun to overhaul and simplify public worship. He had taken the six liturgical books in use since the beginning of the Middle Ages, translated them into English, and unified them into a single book.

Meanwhile, Somerset and the regency council appointed Cranmer and a committee comprised of conservatives, liberals, and moderates to develop an official prayer book for the Church of England. The Houses of Parliament considered their efforts and, in 1549, passed the Act of Uniformity establishing their labors as the Prayer Book of the realm. This first Book of Common Prayer (1549) was fundamentally an English simplification, a condensation of numerous liturgical sources and a reform of the old Latin rites. Still, from the beginning, it was controversial. The conservatives disliked its innovation and the reformers did not believe it went far enough. The pressure was great to make more radical reforms and, in 1552, a new Prayer Book was established that was more Protestant. However, it only lasted eight months and was unpopular with everyone.

When the young King Edward died, Mary, the ardently Roman Catholic daughter of Henry VIII and Catherine of Aragon, assumed the throne. The Latin mass immediately replaced the Book of Common Prayer, medieval Roman Catholic customs and practices resurfaced, and those bishops who had remained faithful to Rome were restored to power. Reconciliation with Rome was sought and the persecution of those who had in any way espoused the reformers' cause began. Cranmer, the Archbishop of Canterbury, and bishops Latimer and Ridley, who had participated in the early liturgical reform movement, were excommunicated and burned at the stake. Nevertheless, Mary's attempt at a Counter-Reformation also ended in disaster.

The Anglican Church Is Born

The Anglican Church as we know it did not come fully into its own until the reign of Elizabeth I, the daughter of Henry and Anne Boleyn. The year was 1558. Elizabeth was twenty-four, and she began a reign that lasted forty-five years and established the foundation of the Anglican Church.

Elizabeth found herself confronted by two hostile groups, Roman Catholics and Protestants, and a third moderate group, small but influential, that intended the Church of England to be truly catholic in all essentials and yet fully cleansed and reformed of medieval abuses. She chose this middle way, which resulted in her being excommunicated and deposed by the Pope in the papal bull of 1570. This marked the final separation of England from Rome.

Her first parliament met and passed two defining acts—a new Act of Supremacy and a new Act of Uniformity. In the first Act of Supremacy, Henry VIII was established as the "supreme head" of the church and state. In this second Act of Supremacy, Elizabeth is named the "supreme governor" of church and state, a change acknowledging that Christ was the true head of the church. In the second Act of Uniformity, a new Book of Common Prayer (1559) was authorized. It made a few changes in the 1549 and 1552 versions to symbolically establish a middle way.

For example, the words used in the administration of the Sacrament in the 1549 Prayer Book were, "The Body (Blood) of our Lord Jesus Christ, which is given (shed) for thee. Preserve thy body and soul unto everlasting life"—a more Roman Catholic understanding. These words were replaced in the 1552 Prayer Book by the words, "Take and eat (drink) this in remembrance that Christ died (Christ's blood was shed) for thee, and feed on him in thy heart by faith, with thanksgiving (and be thankful)"—a more Protestant understanding. In the 1559 Prayer Book, they were combined into a single statement, as you will find them in Rite I of our 1979 Prayer Book.

Nevertheless, the Puritan Calvinists were not satisfied. They rejected the episcopacy and opposed vestments; they were opposed to organs, ecclesial music, ornaments such as processional crosses, and ceremonies such as the sign of the cross at Baptism, the imposition of hands at Confirmation, the ring at marriage, bowing at the name of Jesus, and kneeling at communion.

Elizabeth held strong. The Church of England was to be, as the title page to the first Prayer Book implied, a part of the Catholic Church, but also reformed. The liturgy would be in English, the sacrament would be administered in both kinds, and the clergy would be permitted to marry. The liturgy would be based upon true scholarship, drawing on the best traditions of the early church, faithful to scripture but not limited to scripture, and always inclusive of diversity and dignity.

Still, the Prayer Book was under attack by the Puritans on the left and the Roman Catholics on the right. Keeping the Church of England together were a rejection of uniformity and the principle of unity with diversity, which manifested itself as a loyalty to the Book of Common Prayer and a willingness to support a variety of liturgical practices. For example, some churches used stone altars against the wall and others used freestanding wooden tables in the middle of the assembly; some used unleavened wafers and others leavened bread; some received the Eucharist kneeling and some received standing. There were priests who wore vestments and those who did not. Some churches maintained old wall paintings and processional crosses while others had whitewashed walls and tablets containing the Apostles' Creed, the Lord's Prayer, and the Ten Commandments. Church music was both encouraged and discouraged. Eucharist was celebrated weekly in some parishes and once a month after Morning Prayer in others. Still, in one sense, the Elizabethan compromise, a middle ground between fanatical Puritans and embittered Romans, was never fully accepted. The 1559 Prayer Book and variety of ways it was used were representative of Anglicanism at its best.

Elizabeth died and James I came to the throne. The next month, the Puritans presented him with a petition listing offenses in the 1559 Book of Common Prayer. With the establishment of the 1604 Book of Common Prayer, James went a step further than Elizabeth in that he pronounced excommunication on those, Puritans or Romanists, who refused to use the book. None of the warring parties were satisfied, of course. Still, in 1611, under James I's leadership, forty-seven scholars produced the Authorized or, as it is better known, the King James Version of the Bible.

At the same time, behind the scenes, there were those in the Church of England who were framing and consolidating new understandings and ways to support an emerging tradition. These folk, led by devout, scholarly, and dignified moderates such as Richard Hooker and

Lancelot Andrewes, defended a Church of England that would be fully catholic and reformed. Their writings impressed the king, who had become discontented with Scottish Presbyterianism and suspicious of Roman Catholicism.

Charles I inherited a conviction from his father concerning the Divine Right of Kings and so, in the face of what appeared to be unreasonable tensions between Catholics and Protestants, he asserted his authority by dissolving Parliament and ruled by turning over political authority to the Earl of Statford and church authority to William Laud, the Archbishop of Canterbury. Laud was a bitter opponent of the Puritans and Calvinists and, while following in the footsteps of Hooker, was more Catholic and, like Charles I, an autocrat. For example, he insisted that church altars be placed against an east wall and fenced with an elaborate altar rail. Soon these unpopular actions resulted in a civil war and a brief death of the Book of Common Prayer. The execution of Charles I marked a triumph for Puritanism. Fortunately, however, once again a group of leaders were quietly shaping the future of the Anglican Church; namely, Jeremy Taylor, George Herbert, and Nicholas Ferrar. Once again moderate voices for a truly catholic and reformed church that accepted the principle of being fully catholic and fully Protestant, however difficult that might be, stood firm.

During the Commonwealth, the period of the Cromwellians, the religious life of the country was in great confusion. But once again, followers of a middle way offered hope. With the death of Oliver Cromwell, Charles II, who was in exile, returned to a jubilant welcome, but also to a very delicate situation. Still, the new king was on the side of those who wished to restore the vision of the Anglican Church. A new Prayer Book was adopted in 1662 and with it the Church of England was fully restored. And while there have been numerous reforms since, this Prayer Book remains the official, that is, the foundational, Prayer Book of the Church of England.

The Birth of the United States of America and the Episcopal Church

It was no surprise that the American Revolution necessitated a revision in the English 1662 Book of Common Prayer. There were the obvious changes in the prayers that eliminated mention of the monarch and loyalty to the crown in the ordination rite. But more significant was the influence of the prayer book tradition emerging from the Scottish Episcopal Church, which years before had denied the authority of the Elizabethan Acts of Supremacy and Uniformity as well as the 1559 Prayer Book. Instead, the Scottish bishops, with the help of William Laud, the Archbishop of Canterbury, produced the Scottish book of 1637, a book similar to the more Catholic English book of 1549, which clearly differentiated them from the Scottish Calvinists.

The first American Prayer Book was never popular and it was revised in 1764, at the same time that Samuel Seabury was consecrated as the first bishop in the United States by bishops in the Scottish Episcopal Church. The new Prayer Book, as might be expected, was strongly influenced by the Scottish Prayer Book, but even more so by the newly rediscovered liturgical ways of the early church.

The American church soon found that it also needed to respond to its new social, political, cultural, and theological context. William White and William Smith made an early attempt at a simplified revision of 1662, which was accepted by the southern states, but the 1786 book was not popular in the northern states. Instead, at the first General Convention of the Protestant Episcopal Church in the United States, our first American Prayer Book, the 1789 Book of Common Prayer, more in line with the Scottish book and the new scholarship, was adopted.

A way of life in community was also established. At this organizing convention of the Episcopal Church, proper biblical lessons, psalms, and prayers were established for a proposed observance of Independence Day. But Bishop White, the first Bishop of Pennsylvania, a supporter of the Revolution, chaplain to the Continental Congress, chief architect of the Episcopal Church's Constitution, and presiding bishop at this first General Convention, negotiated to have the day removed from the proposed church calendar as an act of reconciliation with those loyalist clergy who had been persecuted and killed, placed in prison, and driven from their parishes for being loyal to their ordination vow to be loyal to the king. So it was that the celebration of Independence Day in the Episcopal Church did not become part of our liturgical life until the birth of the 1928 Book of Common Prayer.

Our Anglican flip-flopping between the excesses of Romanism and Calvinism and the influence of Luther as well as the extremes of

Laudianism (high church ceremonial) and Puritanism (low church non-ceremonial) had lost enthusiasm. Further, the Latitudinarians had emerged as a significant voice in the life of the church. These descendants of humanism sought toleration, an end to religious controversy, and a more inclusive church; thus, a "broad church," where reasonableness was dominant, had its influence on the American Prayer Book. Even the subtle name of the church, "Protestant" (not Roman) "Episcopal" (not Protestant), gave evidence to this new-old middle way. In many ways the name was conservative and restrained, but it was accepted and survived a hundred years.

Controversy continues over such issues as the use of the Apostles' Creed or the Nicene Creed, the inclusion or removal of the phrase "he descended into hell," the style of church architecture, and various liturgical practices including Morning Prayer or Holy Eucharist on Sunday. The plea for greater flexibility is heard and moderate changes are made here and there. Significantly, over time, liturgical decisions moved from monarchs, archbishops, and scholars to clergy, bishops, and scholars; finally, they included the laity.

In 1892, the Prayer Book was modestly revised, establishing the principle that future liturgical reform was both necessary and possible. Worship and daily life and work could not be separated, and changes in our political, economic, and social world had to be reflected in our worship. And, so far as we acknowledge that the "rule of prayer is the rule of believing," changes in theology, ethics, and spirituality need to be reflected in our worship. Such convictions not only led to the 1928 Book of Common Prayer but to the establishment of the Liturgical Standing Committee, a committee of General Convention comprised of clergy and laity assigned responsibility to continue the revision and expansion of the Book of Common Prayer into the future.

The 1928 revision was more dramatic than previous revisions. While some loved it and others did not, from the beginning it too was a book in need of revision. The liturgical movement and the ecumenical movement had begun and would affect all of Christendom. Their roots were in the Reformation and would prove as radical. Modernity, which began in the sixteenth century, was ending, as did the medieval synthesis in the sixteenth. Biblical, theological, liturgical, and spiritual scholarship was expanding our understanding and practice of liturgy. Social, economic, political, racial, and cultural realities were in upheaval. Grassroots groups such as the "Associated Parishes for Liturgy and Mission" were founded and fostered experimentation and implementation of insights from the liturgical movement. The dramatic changes that came with the Second Vatican Council affected even the Anabaptists, the most radical of Protestant reformers.

All of this resulted in the 1979 Book of Common Prayer. While some have still not accepted it and some do not yet use it as intended, it is a book in progress. While it emerged over time through trial liturgies and democratic procedures, it never pleased everyone. Indeed, there has been a small movement to reestablish the 1928 book. While I am convinced that the 1979 Prayer Book has made an immensely important contribution to our faith and life, more reform, I believe, is necessary.

Last Thoughts

Reform is already underway. For many Episcopalians, this will not be good news; surely, new controversies will emerge. But we have a long history of similar conflicts. I hope that this brief overview will help you to put everything in perspective and enable us to learn from the past how to remain united and affirm diversity.

There have always been those who have looked back to either a Protestant or Catholic understanding of the Christian life of faith and its relationship to the church's liturgy. We will never produce the ideal Prayer Book, even for some particular historic period. We may argue that diversity will destroy unity or unity will destroy diversity, but the Anglican way is to mediate these two principles at all cost. Such a position will make both continuity with the past and change for the future possible and fruitful. As in every social system, we will always need to conserve the past, but to survive we must always adapt to a new possibility.

The issues, of course, have changed from Catholic-Protestant debates to inclusivity in terms of race, ethnicity, gender orientation, and culture. There are also ecumenical concerns such as the new Revised Common Lectionary, a change in the wording of the Nicene Creed that will make it consistent with the earliest version still used by Eastern Orthodox Christians, new eucharistic prayers and roles of clergy and laity. Newly approved liturgical texts and an expanded *Book of Occasional Services* are on the horizon.

For example, we will need to begin reflecting on the question: What will it mean to be a people of a book when, instead of a bound book, congregations will print user-friendly disposable leaflets for particular liturgies from an ever-changing and expanding library of resources? Our understanding of unity will change from being centered on a book with covers approved for use by the church to the establishment of standards for texts and agreed upon structures for our rituals such as we find in 1979 Prayer Book "Rite for Celebration of the Eucharist." Of one thing we can be sure. We will always have a resource known as the Book of Common Prayer and it will always be changing to meet new needs and new historical conditions. And I suspect some will like and some will not like the changes and additions or corrections made over time. There will also always be diversity in how we celebrate our various rituals. I hope that we will be able to maintain unity with diversity as we have in the past. Knowing about our history and the development of our Prayer Book over time should give us hope and inspire us to continue the process of adaptation and change.

What has been established throughout our history is the assumption that theological and ethical issues needed to be addressed through our liturgical life. We shape our understanding of faith and life through participation in our liturgies. We reflect on our convictions about faith and life by reflecting on our liturgies. And we reform our understandings and ways of life by revising our present liturgies and by creating new ones.

Importantly, from the beginning we have been a people committed to live by the principle of comprehensiveness or the *via media* (literally, nothing too much or the middle way). This principle is founded on the conviction that truth is best understood as maintaining the tension between what may appear to be two counter-opposites; for example, Jesus is fully human and fully divine and the church is to be both catholic and Protestant. For example, at the time of the Reformation the Roman Catholic Church taught that people needed to do a lot after Baptism to achieve salvation. The Protestant reformers taught that we needed to do nothing after Baptism to achieve salvation. Our Anglican theologians sought a middle way, teaching that Baptism establishes who and whose we are as a saved people, but then tells us that we need to spend the rest of our lives striving to become who we already are as a saved people.

The church is called to be a community of faith so that it might become the body of Christ, God's presence and action in the world. As the body of Christ, the church is called to be a missional church. That is, we are not called to have a mission but to be a mission, to be an embodiment of God's grace, a sign and witness to what it means to abide in the reign of God. However, to be a missional church we need to be a community of faith, a community bound together by a common story, a common ritual, a common authority, a common life more like a family than an institution, and a common end other than survival. But at our heart and soul we will always be a people of a prayer book, ever the same and ever changing, but always a story-formed people.

CHAPTER 3
LIVING AS A STORY-FORMED PEOPLE

⸌⸍

At first it may seem strange that, after a brief preface and a few comments concerning the worship of the church in the Book of Common Prayer, we find eighteen pages containing a calendar for the church year. However, on further reflection, it makes sense. This calendar is not just a collection of dates; it an outline of the sacred narrative that comprises the foundation for the Christian life of faith

Richard Adams's novel *Watership Down,* ostensibly an adventure story about rabbits, is really about the conditions necessary for a viable community, namely, the ability to sustain the narrative that defines its life. *Watership Down* begins with an exodus, a hazardous journey in search of a new home, ultimately, Watership Down. The rabbits move out as a group of separate individuals, each with his or her own reasons for leaving. They become a people, a community, as they acquire a story. And they remain a community so long as they retell their story.

So it is with us. Our identity is dependent on having a story that tells us who we are. Our understanding of life's meaning and purpose is dependent on having a story that tells us what the world is like and where we are going. To be a community of faith, we must be a people with a story: a common memory and vision, common rituals or symbolic actions expressive of our community's memory and vision, and a common life together that manifests our community's memory and vision.

The church is a story-formed community. Baptism is our adoption into a story, God's story, which is recorded in the community's storybook (the Bible), incarnate in the community's life, and made present through its sacramental rituals. Each of us also has a personal story, and our aim is to make God's story and our stories one story. In the context of our liturgies, we are initiated into God's story and we appropriate its significance for our lives so that it might influence our common life day by day. And as we journey through history and traverse life-cycle passages, the retelling of God's story sustains us and moves us along.

There are those who have difficulty understanding that the Bible is fundamentally a storybook and that the calendar of the church year provides us with an outline of that story. Of course, there are those who reject this notion and understand the Bible as a collection of proof texts for doctrinal truths and moral convictions rather than a storybook to be dramatized and lived out within a story-formed community. Sacred stories are symbolic stories, never to be taken literally. As symbolic stories they point beyond themselves and participate in a truth otherwise unavailable to us.

The church did not collect the stories in the Bible to create a theological or ethical textbook. While theological and ethical systems can and need to emerge out of scripture, scripture must first and foremost be understood as sacred narrative and poetic truth. Stories resist any definitive interpretation and invite diverse and ever new commentaries. Theology is abstract, but not story; story invites participation. We discuss theology but we experience story. Theological speculation limits and divides; story frees and unites. Only adults can engage in meaningful theological reflection; stories are for all ages. "Tell me a story" is the request of every child. At the heart of the Christian faith is story, not dogma.

The major roles in Peter Shaffer's play *Equus* are an adolescent boy and his psychiatrist. The young man has blinded a number of horses after being seduced by a woman employee of the stable. The psychiatrist's task is to analyze the cause of this psychotic behavior and free the young man for productive life. What is unveiled in the drama is the mental torment of a patient and the story he developed to make it tolerable. The psychiatrist comments, "We need a story to see in the dark." We all need such a story. Stories are the means by which we see reality. Without a story, it would appear as if we lived in an unreal world. Without a story, we cannot live. Without a story, we cannot have community. In the beginning is a story that provides us with both a memory linking us meaningfully with the past and a vision calling us to a purposeful future. Without a story, life makes no sense. The story that is foundational to our life provides us with the basis for our perceptions and for our faith. Faith is manifested in story; story communicates faith. Anyone familiar with Chaucer's *Canterbury Tales* will remember that the pilgrims told stories on the way to the shrine of St. Thomas à Becket. Stories are the imaginative way of ordering our experience. The pilgrimage of life requires a story.

The Nature of Story

Stories are concrete and particular. Stories are open-ended. They are not to be taken literally; in fact, stories give the storyteller freedom in their retelling. Stories stimulate the imagination. There is never only one interpretation of a story; indeed, the listener is encouraged to listen freely and discover personal meaning. Stories are experiential. A participant tells them, and they are to be participated in. Stories are the bottom line of human communal life: Ultimately, nothing else is needed.

The Bible is a storybook. Basically, it is a love story between God and humanity; a story of a covenant made, broken, and renewed, again and again. The triune God, whose nature and character is to love, creates, redeems, and perfects human life and history. And we are expected to love God, ourselves, each other, and God's creation, as God loves.

We need to enlarge our grasp of this love story—to learn it more completely, to understand it more deeply, to possess it more personally, and to live it more fully. This is a lifelong task. While it is important that we make reading, studying, and meditating upon the Bible a regular part of our lives, most important is our participation in the story through worship in church.

As we prepare to explore this sacred narrative, it will be important to remember that, before the era known as the Enlightenment beginning in the seventeenth century, there were two accepted approaches to reality and truth. One was called "mythos" and the other "logos." Mythos involved the intuitive way of thinking and knowing. Nurtured by the arts, it focused on the imagination. Mythos manifested itself through symbols, myths, and rituals. Logos involved the intellectual way of thinking and knowing. Nurtured by the sciences, it focused on rational propositions and rational principles. Logos manifested itself in ideas, facts, and history. However, as the Age of Reason emerged, mythos lost its place of influence and the search for truth emphasized the need to demythologize the Bible. Those who opposed this histori- cal critical approach to the Bible turned mythos into logos, thereby turning the creation myth into literal scientific fact, known as cre- ationism. We need to return to the earlier understanding of mythos and to an acknowledgment of the important role myth plays in sacred narrative. Our challenge today is to re-mythologize the Bible.

A myth is a metaphorical or symbolic narrative. Myths are "really true" even though they may or may not be literally or factually true. Mythic language is the language of faith in that myths provide us with a way to see or perceive reality that otherwise is hidden or not self-evi- dent. Myths point beyond themselves to the presence and action of God in human life and history; that is, they are sacramental.

In *The Dark Interval: Toward a Theology of Story,*[1] John Dominic Crossan offers a fivefold typology of sacred stories, namely: myth, apo- logue, action, satire, and parable. While each serves a different and unique function, myths and parables are foundational to the life of faith.

The function of myth is to establish our world. Myths explain that this is the way life really is, in spite of any evidence to the contrary. Myths are not false stories. In fact, as the Pawnee Indians were wise to point out, it is history that is composed of false stories; myths are true stories because they are about God; they are more than history in that they point beyond history to its meaning. The stories of Jesus' birth and resurrection are myths. They explain the nature and character of God and the meaning and purpose of life and death. They are true sto- ries in the most important sense of those words, for they explain our world. Everyone lives by some collection of myths. No one finds mean- ing or purpose in life without them.

Apologetic stories defend our myths. They are primarily biograph- ical in nature, for what better defense is there for a particular way of envisioning life than the lives of those who believe it and live by it? It is difficult to argue with the person who is willing to suffer and die for a particular way of understanding life and its meaning. The testimonies of the apostles, including Paul, are good examples. That also is why the stories of the saints, the ancient and modern heroes of the faith, are also important to know and share.

Action or narrative stories explore the world that our myths estab- lish and the biographies defend. For example, our myth may tell us that God is a merciful and loving God, but our experience may indicate otherwise. Narratives explore these contradictions and in the end reaffirm the myth. The story of Job is a perfect example.

Satire serves to attack our worldview. For example, consider the story of Jonah in which Jonah believes that God's justice is for retribution, but God reveals his justice as reconciliation.

Lastly, there are parables whose function is to subvert the way our culture sees life so that we might perceive the world in ways consistent with our myths. For example, consider Jesus' story of the vineyard: God does not give us what we deserve but what we need. That is consistent with the Christian myth of a gracious and merciful God, but it is subversive to those of us who live in a reward-and-punishment world. This world defines justice as getting what you deserve and has difficulty supporting welfare for fear people will get something they do not deserve.

Of course, there is other material in the Bible, such as prophetic judgments on persons and communities whose lives violate the implications of the community's myths. There are songs and prayers that celebrate life as it is lived within the context of our myths, and there are words of wisdom gleaned from experience that support the community's myth. But the heart of the Bible is a love story—the Christian myth—that must be known, owned, and lived if we are to be Christians.

Southern novelist Walker Percy wrote an essay entitled "The Message in the Bottle."[2] He asks us to imagine a man shipwrecked on an island with no recollection of who he is or where his home is. The castaway is warmly received by the islanders, who, he discovers, have a remarkably advanced culture with highly developed social institutions. While in time he becomes assimilated into their culture and a useful member of the society, he remains uncomfortable. Wanting to know who he is and where he came from, he wanders the beach each morning to mediate on his situation. He occasionally finds bottles that have been washed up on the shore. In each is a single piece of paper with a brief message. Some are trivial, some nonsensical; some state falsehoods as fact; some are informational and important to life on the island, for example, identifying fresh water in the next cove.

In time, he discovers that the messages can be divided into two quite different groups: "pieces of knowledge" and "pieces of news." The pieces of knowledge, while of some value, only contain information that, while changeable, is generally available to everyone. News, on the other hand, is not only important, but also especially relevant to the needs and predicaments of the islanders. And it is, of course, important to know the difference.

Nevertheless, the message he longs for is not a message that will only make life in the island culture possible. It is a message from across the sea that will tell him who he is and where he came from so that his life on the island might have meaning and purpose.

This message is the gospel story. This sacred story is not objective knowledge discoverable by anyone, anywhere, at any time. It is a special form of good news that tells us about ourselves and our predicament. It reveals to us who we are and where our true homeland is to be found.

I am convinced that this is the true nature and character of Holy Scripture. When we turn the canon of scripture into knowledge, knowledge about doctrine, propositional truths, or moral practices, we make a grave error.

Stories are oral and communal in nature. They are meant to be told, dramatized, sung, danced, and expressed through the visual arts. We forget that our biblical story was written down only because the community was worried that its storytellers might forget, distort, or neglect some important aspect of them. In order that our stories may, as intended, shape our lives, we need to make them foundational to our life of faith.

Rituals, like stories, emerge from and speak to our intuitive, emotional consciousness. That explains why dance, drama, music, and the visual arts are the means by which our rituals are best enacted. It also explains why the language of poetry is more basic than discursive prose in our rituals. When worship becomes too intellectual or wordy, it loses its depth and significance.

One of the problems in Western culture, especially post-Reformation Enlightenment culture, is that it is ocular in nature; that is, it is a book-oriented culture that reads and writes. We speak of the "eyes of faith" and hold that "seeing is believing." We are wordy and our preaching is discursive. We turn sacred stories into historical events and doctrinal statements. We encourage people to turn the biblical story into pornography (a subject turned into an object for our investigation and manipulation) or idolatry (a proper means turned into an end). In an oral culture, the learning of stories involve all the senses and the imagination as well. In an oral culture, truth is poetic and storytelling is understood as the doorway into the realm of the sacred. People living in an oral culture experience life holistically, integrated and inter-connected. The biblical stories become a sacred narrative that is to be imagined and participated in, not studied objectively or believed liter-ally. Oral cultures understand that rituals are symbolic actions that manifest and express the community's sacred story. Through these rit-uals the community preserves its memory of past events, anticipates future events, and makes sense out of life in the present.

Ritual provides the means by which we humans are enabled to live in two interrelated worlds: the world of outward events or material reality and the world of inner experience or nonmaterial reality. To be human is to integrate the inner world of imagination, intuition, and subjective experience with the outer world of interpretive, intellectual, objective reflection and moral action.

For Christians, the canon of Holy Scripture is essentially a story, a revelatory sacred narrative that is intended to be incorporated into our personal and communal stories. Holy Scripture is not an end in itself. To make it such is an act of idolatry. Idolatry is turning that which is intended to be a means into an end. Holy Scripture is best understood as the means by which it is revealed to us who and whose we are and therefore how we are to live in relationship to God, to each other, and to the natural world.

One interesting way to integrate the biblical story with our story is to acquire a copy of *Lesser Feasts and Fasts* (New York: Church Pub-lishing, 2003) and develop a spiritual discipline based upon its days of remembrance. For example, May 8 is the feast of Dame Julian of Nor-wich, who died in 1417. To help you prayerfully reflect on her life and how it might relate to yours, you will find a brief statement about the significance of her life and faithfulness. Rather than trying to compare your life with hers, be quiet and ponder if the story of her life can pro-vide you with any insights into your own. For me, it is not her mystic life as an anchoress that draws my interest, but rather her awareness of the all-embracing, never-ending, unconditional, unmerited love of God.

You will also find a collect, a prayer whose purpose is to focus our minds on some particular characteristic of the person we are asked to remember. In the case of Julian, we are reminded of our need to acknowledge that the one end of all human life is to grow in an ever deepening and loving relationship with God; all else is intended to be means. This might be a good time to write a prayerful letter to God about your difficulties and accomplishments, your successes and failures, closing with a request for the particular help of God that you need to live more faithfully in relationship with God.

Each of the entries includes a recommended psalm as well as two lessons from scripture for meditation. In Julian's case, Psalm 27:5–14, Hebrews 10:19–24, and John 4:23–26 are included. Read and meditate on each—not as if they were intended to give you knowledge of doctrine you must believe or moral practices you must emulate. Rather, prayerfully reflect on them to discover what they might reveal about who and whose you are and how you are to live in relationship with God, yourself, all others, and God's creation.

Then let the "message in the bottle" surface from the appointed psalm and the stories of God's faithfulness in the excerpt from the Letter to the Hebrews. We need never live in fear. God can be trusted to keep God's promises. We can have hope in God's love. The underlying story in the brief passage from John's gospel is that our response is to worship God accordingly, in spirit and in truth.

You might prayerfully ponder the implications of this message of good news by asking yourself how this message contributes to your understanding of life and of your own life. Ask yourself: How might I live differently if I took this message with ultimate seriousness?

Most importantly, we need to let the biblical story inform and shape our lives, just as it has shaped the character and content of our Book of Common Prayer.

CHAPTER 4

LIVING AS A PILGRIM PEOPLE

The church is a story-formed community, a people on pilgrimage through time, through seasons of profane time made holy by the eternal cycle of sacred time. The manner in which we order and use time is the best indicator of what is important to us. Time both expresses and shapes our lives. We live in time. We find time for what we consider important, and how we spend our time influences our understandings and ways of life. We recall and celebrate the occasions that are most significant to us, and the days we celebrate give meaning and purpose to our lives.

There are, of course, those churches whose time is occupied with various promotional events, much like the calendar of a department store: Stewardship Sunday, Children's Day, Missionary Sunday, Evangelism Sunday, and the like. Institutional maintenance seems to be their primary concern. And there are those churches that celebrate only birthdays and forget baptism days, and make more of Rally Day, Mother's Day, Thanksgiving Day, and Independence Day than they do of the Transfiguration, Ascension Day, Holy Cross Day, the festival of the Holy Innocents, and various saints' days. Nevertheless, it is the eternal cycle of the church year with its re-presentation of God's story in interaction with our human story that best orders our lives within a Christian faith community. One of the fundamental aims of liturgy is to help us to relive God's story in such a way that it touches, illumines, and transforms our human story and thereby shapes our lives to serve

God's purposes for personal and communal life. In our case, that implies our relating God's story to our human stories as we travel together through the eternal cycle of sacred time as celebrated in the church year. Our sharing of a personal pilgrimage through a year in the church's liturgical life is intended to stimulate our imaginations and touch our hearts and minds as pilgrims who choose to travel each year over the same route in search of meaning and purpose.

A Pilgrim's Tale

In the Book of Common Prayer 1979, directly before the rite for Holy Baptism, we find a section entitled "Proper Liturgies for Special Days." These correspond to the earliest liturgies celebrated in the church. The significance of these liturgical observances lies in their beauty and theological depth as well as in the drama they offer of universal conflictual themes: light versus darkness, truth versus error, and good versus evil, along with our common human experiences of betrayal, abandonment, injustice, compassion, redemptive suffering, and new life. Within this one week, beginning with the Sunday of the Passion, Palm Sunday, our minds are boggled, our hearts quickened, and our wills stirred. At the heart of the week is the Triduum, the three most holy days in the church year. Regretfully, too many neglect to participate in these sacred liturgies. Consequently, they may find it difficult to fully understand or commit themselves to the Christian life of faith.

Nevertheless, each year we begin our participation in the church's sacred drama with a eucharistic liturgy, "The Sunday of the Passion: Palm Sunday," that is theologically complex and personally compelling because it casts us personally and communally as members of a crowd that can both acclaim Jesus as the Christ who is ushering in God's reign and demand his death as a criminal of the state.

We begin by being called to represent the moving experience of "entering with joy upon the contemplation of those mighty acts whereby God has given us life and immortality." A gospel about the first Palm Sunday is read, the palms are blessed, and the meaning of the event and its symbols is laid out in prayer. The blessed palms are distributed and the process begins as we all exclaim, "Blessed is the one who comes in the name of the Lord. Hosanna in the highest." But soon after we enter the church, the mood of the liturgy changes dramatically. The crosses in the church are veiled in red as symbolic death shrouds and the theme becomes Christ's passion. In the midst of hearing the passion narrative, we scream out, "Crucify him."

During the first three days of Holy Week, it is appropriate to celebrate the Way of the Cross and Tenebrae, which you will find in *The Book of Occasional Services,* the official addendum to the Book of Common Prayer. The Way of the Cross is an adaptation of a custom practiced by pilgrims in Jerusalem that tells the story of God's redemptive acts on behalf of a fallen humanity as they unfold in the last hours of Jesus' life. Focusing on Jesus and his mother, these fourteen "stations" are based on both biblical and nonbiblical traditions, as each offers devotional readings, time for meditation in silence, prayers, and solemn songs associated with Christ's passion and death.

The most conspicuous feature of Tenebrae is the gradual extinguishing of candles until only a single candle, a symbol of Christ, remains. Toward the end of the liturgy, the candle is hidden, symbolizing the apparent victory of evil. At the very end, after the singing of Psalm 51, a loud noise is made symbolizing the earthquake at the time of the resurrection, the hidden candle is restored to its place, and the congregation departs.

Now comes the Triduum liturgies, which begin after sunset on Thursday and extend to sunset on Sunday. The liturgies of the Triduum focus on the Eucharist as the Lord's Passover meal, on the redemptive death of Jesus that makes possible a new life of faith, on the sacrament of Baptism through which we are incorporated into the death and resurrection of Jesus and made members of his body, and on the resurrection of the historical Jesus.

We begin with the Vigil of Good Friday, commonly known as Maundy Thursday. A series of conflicting realities will impinge on one another this night. The church is made most beautiful with white hangings, flowers, and white veils on its crosses, in stark contrast to Lent with its penitential purple hangings, the elimination or covering of gold crosses, and the absence of flowers. We sing for the first time since Ash Wednesday the "Gloria in excelsis" in honor of Jesus' institution of the Eucharist during his last supper with his friends. The word "Maundy" is derived from the Latin for "command," and as we wash each other's feet as Jesus had done with his friends, we recall that this symbolic act is to remind us of Jesus' intention that we who chose to follow him will love ourselves and all others as he loved us. That is, we will live as a reconciled and reconciling community, which is the purpose and hope of our making Eucharist together. Following communion, there is a stripping of the altar and the removal of all liturgical and decorative items. This experience of contrasts is overwhelming. But then comes the dramatic action of taking whatever consecrated bread and wine remains and, as we are reminded of the gospel account of his disciples struggling to keep watch with him in the garden, process it to a chapel or a place where members of the parish may keep watch all night with Christ. During this watch, we meditate on Jesus' struggle to discern God's will and on our need to do the same in terms of those things to which we need to die if we are to be faithful.

Good Friday follows. Good Friday is at the heart of the Christian faith, not because of Christ's torturous death, but because of what it demonstrates about the character of God, God who loves us so much that God is willing to suffer and die so that we might know the nature of God's unconditional, unmerited, unending, forgiving, reconciling love. Therefore, on Good Friday we focus on the adoration of the cross or on our response to God's gracious love.

Having buried our crucified Lord, on Holy Saturday we recall that he descended into hell, to that state or condition chosen by those who have through their actions estranged themselves from God, from their true self, from others, and from God's creation. We remember that God never has and never will give up on those who have chosen to live estranged lives. Even God's judgment is for reconciliation, not retribution. God's wrath is about God's anger tempered by God's mercy and love. God goes to them and shares in their pain with the hope that they will be moved by his love and return.

And then we enter into the Great Vigil of Easter. With a focus on Baptism and the renewal of our baptismal vows and covenant, we celebrate Christ's resurrection. Easter exists because of Good Friday, not in spite of Good Friday. Good Friday does not focus on what evil people did to Jesus that God overcomes, but on how the birth of new life is the consequence of Christ's death. Beginning in darkness, then with the lighting of a new fire and the processional of a new paschal candle, we recall the story of salvation. And as dawn breaks, we celebrate the resurrection. While there is no celebration of the Eucharist, communion is offered from the reserved sacrament that has been in the chapel of repose. At the completion of this liturgy, all the consecrated elements are consumed so that there is no reserved sacrament. The day concludes with the Great Vigil of Easter, the most important celebration in the church year.

As an Episcopalian who had never participated in these liturgical experiences, I found myself many years ago as a consultant to our national education staff in New York. We appropriately took time off each day for worship. I chose to attend services each day from the Vigil of Good Friday to the Vigil of Easter at St. Mary the Virgin. That experience transformed my understanding of the Christian life of faith. In every parish I have been in since then, I have done my best to initiate these services and convince people to participate in all of them. Universally, those who have done so have acknowledged that this experience has significantly affected their lives more than any other experience they have ever had in the church. So let me simply say, do whatever you can to have this experience. Our gospel faith will come alive for you as never before.

A Pilgrimage through the Church Year

Good Friday to Easter

If we consider our story solely from a historical perspective, we would begin with Advent. But doing so can distort the story. From the perspective of Christian faith, the story begins and ends with Good Friday through Easter. The mystery of faith that we proclaim is: "Christ has died, Christ is risen, Christ will come again."

It is important to remember that God's Friday, Great Friday, Good Friday cannot be separated from Easter. Knowing that to suffer is to be human, on that Friday God chose to suffer with us so that we might know how much God loves us in spite of everything we do to be unlovable. Christ's death upon the cross is also the means God had established, from the beginning, to conquer evil through the power of suffering love, a power the world labels weakness.

Just as it is not appropriate to celebrate the Way or Stations of the Cross on Good Friday, the typical Protestant Good Friday three-hour liturgy, I believe, can miss the point of the day. The Good Friday service in the Prayer Book is quite different. It has three dimensions: 1) the service of the Word in which we confront the meaning of the passion; 2) the adoration of the cross by which we respond in love to God's act of love; and 3) the reception of communion, which is a consummation of all the consecrated bread and wine that had been reserved after the Maundy Thursday Eucharist, thereby making Christ no longer present in our midst—that is, until Easter and the resurrection.

The point of Easter is that the crucified one lives, precisely as the crucified one. Good Friday is a day of sorrow, but not sadness, for in the mystery of the crucifixion we are able to see God's sacrificial love that delivers the world from the power of evil. In the resulting joy of Easter, we celebrate a dream come true, a vision become reality, the fullness of life made present, the intentions of creation fulfilled, the sovereign reign of God established. Here our story both begins and ends.

At the Vigil of Easter we gather in the dark of morning to light a new fire, to light from it a new paschal candle, to process into the church with our candles lighted off the paschal candle, to sing the *Exultet* (the fourth-century proclamation of the mysteries of this holy night), to hear the whole story of salvation (the creation of the world, the flood, the deliverance from the Red Sea, and numerous prophesies that set the stage for the drama of redemption), to baptize, especially adults, into the life of the church (and, if there are no candidates for baptism, the congregation will still renew its baptismal vows and covenant), to announce the resurrection, and to celebrate the first Eucharist of Easter together.

While the services of Easter Day that announce the beginning of a new season in the church year (Eastertide or the great fifty days of Easter) are filled with exuberant worshippers, there are no unusual liturgical elements. While the sound of trumpets, the great hymns, exalted music from the choirs, and powerful preaching make this day especially joyful, it is not really different than every other Sunday of the year. Indeed, every Sunday is known as a little Easter.

Before we continue with the story, let us go back to the early church and its worship. The earliest Christians celebrated the Jewish Sabbath, a day of rest or leisure that, unlike work, is its own end. It was a day they either went to the Temple in Jerusalem or, if they lived outside Jerusalem, to a synagogue (meeting house) for instruction and common prayer. Then they also celebrated Sunday, the first day of the week, as the new Christian day of worship—the day of Christ's resurrection. In the context of a ritual meal, they typically held this liturgy on Saturday night after sunset. In time, these two ritual acts of worship were united and moved to Sunday morning, the Christian Sabbath. Sunday Eucharist, a solemn memorial of Christ's death and resurrection, together with the Easter Triduum, formed the earliest festival celebrations in Christianity.

Eastertide

The great fifty days of Easter are intended to be the most joyous and festive days in the whole year. We sing and live the story of a new world of possibility. God's longed-for, hoped-for reign has begun. The true condition of our world is justice and peace, freedom and equity, the unity and well-being of all. Evil still exists, but its power over us is no longer ultimate. Injustice, war, oppression, inequality, division, and poverty still exist, but they are a denial and a distortion of the world's true condition. We live between the already and the not yet, between what is and what is yet to be. God's reign has come, is coming, and will come. We do not need to build God's reign, we need only to abide in it, that is, to live as if it is already within and among us, thereby cooperating with God until it comes in its fullness.

In the early church, those who were baptized at the Easter Vigil wore white garments and during these fifty days after Easter stood with the bishop at the altar for the eucharistic prayer. They also received special instruction in the great mysteries of the faith and the story upon which it is founded. This period was known as the honeymoon of their new life in Christ. And so the great fifty days of Easter became the honeymoon season of the church's year. Now the faithful are encouraged to stand instead of kneeling for prayers and communion, and prayers of confession are eliminated from the liturgy. For fifty glorious days, we sing and dance, party and celebrate a dream come true, a vision made reality, eternal life, God's story brought to fulfillment.

Ascension

Eastertide draws to a close, the party season of the church year is about to end, the honeymoon is almost over, Ascension Day has arrived. There is no more paradoxical day in the year, for on this day we celebrate two conflicting aspects of our story. On the one hand, we sing Alleluia and celebrate Christ's return to God in a glorious, spectacular ascension into the heavens. But the down side that we are to remember is that before he leaves, Jesus says to his disciples, "You are now my body, my presence in the world, but for a time you will be impotent, powerless" (see Luke 24:49ff.). Jesus also promised that the spirit of potency, God's life-giving Spirit, would be given them in God's good time. So it is that our story reminds us that we humans are not in control and can never be in control. We are dependent creatures whose only hope is in God's Spirit. This is where our story and God's story intersect so dramatically. It is one thing to celebrate Christ in glory; it is another to realize that we are now his body on earth. It is one thing to celebrate the power of God that takes Jesus up into heaven; it is another to realize our powerlessness. Nevertheless, we acknowledge on Ascension Day that God has the power to make us powerful and will send his Holy Spirit to empower us, which explains why on this day we are so joyous.

Pentecost

Pentecost is the story of both the gift of God's spirit of potency and its consequence—the birth of the church. Christ's body now has life in and through the Spirit. At Pentecost, God's promised Spirit enters into the church and empowers it to know and do God's will. Now the people of faith can be a sign and witness to what God has done in Christ, namely, established God's reign of justice and peace. On this holy day we are made aware of our vocation to be a community of faith in which God's reconciling power is made present, conscious, and active in our lives, that we might be the body of Christ, God's reconciling presence in the world to the end that all people are restored to unity with God and each other in Christ.

In the Anglican Church, Whitsunday (Pentecost), with Christmas and Easter, ranks among the great feasts of Christianity (see Acts 2:1–4). It commemorates not only the descent of the Holy Spirit, typically represented by a dove inspired by the gospel report of Christ's baptism (Luke 3:21–22), and indicates the fiftieth day after Easter, when the Jews traditionally celebrated their great festival of thanksgiving; it also celebrates the fruits and effects of the coming of God's Holy Spirit. The English word Whitsunday (White Sunday) originated because the newly baptized appeared in white garments on this day, the second feast day for baptisms. In the Western church, the color of liturgical vests is red, symbolizing the love of the Holy Spirit, who descended upon the apostles in tongues of fire.

    With this event, God's story reaches its climax. Half the church year
is over. The following Sundays have always been called the Sundays
after Pentecost. The season is also referred to as "ordinary time,"
because we turn now to a host of short stories intended to aid us understand how we are to live as a people formed by God's story. For six
months we will explore the implications of Good Friday and Easter
and strive to live into our baptisms, to become who we already are, to
be faithful bearers of God's good-news story, the story of God's
redemptive entering into our human lives and history, and of our vocation to live so that all others will know what God has made true for
them also.

All Saints

In the midst of the weeks after Pentecost, in this ordinary time, we celebrate All Saints' Day to remind ourselves and each other that through
our baptism we have been washed clean of sin and made saints, holy
and whole, perfect people, examples of God's intention for all human
beings. Of course, we will continue to fall into sin, but more importantly, we remain saints who sin. Our sin, therefore, is in our denials
and distortions of what God has done and who we are really.

    This is also a time to reflect on the stories of all those named saints
in ages past, those whose personal stories we remember during the
church year. They are remembered because they had some special qual-
ity in their lives, named in the collect for each saint's day, that we are
called upon and can, with God's help, emulate. We are members of this
community of saints, all the baptized, with whom we pray and sing
and with whom one day we will be reunited for eternity.

    In the beginning, All Saints' Day was the feast day for all the mar-
tyrs of the faith. Over time it became a day to celebrate the lives of all
those who the church had established were saints and who lived with
Christ in heaven and could intercede for us and for those in purgatory. The next day, All Souls' Day, was a day to remember all those who
had died and were living in purgatory.

    Much has changed over the years. We Anglicans now celebrate the
lives of all the baptized on All Saints' Day as we remember the lives of
all the faithful departed. On All Souls' Day, we remember the lives of
all those who are not baptized and those whose faith is known to God
alone. During the year we also remember those whose lives were in

some way exemplary, those whom the church has chosen to include in our book of *Lesser Feasts and Fasts*. On their day we celebrate their faithful witness to the gospel, but we do not pray for them to intercede for us as if they were superior to others who are by their baptism also saints.

We, of course, also believe in the communion of the saints, which implies that we can pray for all who have died, they can pray for us, and we can pray together. Therefore, it is a custom for us to visit the burial sites of those we love to pray for and with them on the eve of All Saints' Day. Regretfully, Halloween, a day never connected with any Christian celebration, has occupied and distorted the vigil of All Saints' Day, an opportunity, known as All Hallows' Eve, to prepare for this holy occasion.

It may be difficult to redeem the festival of All Saints and the role of all the baptized in God's plan for the redemption of the world and to remember God's covenant of love with all humanity, but it will help if we place this holy day in the context of our story.

Advent

Six months is a long time to focus on the Christian life of faith. We need to recollect the story that informs and makes possible this way of life, or our pilgrimage of living into our baptism will lose its vitality. After this much time, the dream fades, the vision dulls, and we get weary in well doing. The story that is intended to shape our lives recedes from our consciousness and our faith grows dim. And so we return to the story that begins and ends at Good Friday to Easter by entering into a contemplative, pregnant season of watching expectantly, living prepared, waiting patiently, and giving up control.

Advent reminds us of God's threefold coming: in the past of a baby born in a manger; in the present, in the Holy Scriptures, the sacraments, and life in the church; and in the future by the return of the crucified and risen Jesus to fulfill God's promise. The focus of the story during Advent is, therefore, on preparing for God's future coming and the fulfillment of God's promises.

Advent is the story of hope, the possibility of birth and new life, a rekindled vision to which we are to give our lives. To remember this story makes us uncomfortable with the secular world's celebration of Christmas, a story that has no place for Good Friday to Easter. Advent is a strange, contemplative season to be grasped in the language of silence and poetry. It is time to remember that what we long for and desire has already come and yet is to come in its fullness; a time to remember that we in our day are to be like Mary, to consent to cooperate with God so that God might complete what God began long ago. Her virginity gives us hope by helping us to see that God creates out of nothing and that with God nothing is impossible.

Let us remember that, just as Holy Week required both a season of preparation and a season of celebration, so does Christmas, especially for Anglicans. For us, the incarnation, God's entering our human life and history, has played a special role; thus, our understanding of Advent has been somewhat different. While the Eastern church had no preparation season, the Western church created a festive, joyful season of preparation that in time became a penitential season similar to Lent.

The Anglican Church chose a middle ground, changing the Advent vestment from purple or black like Lent to sursum blue. Advent became a contemplative season to remember with joy and anticipation Christ's threefold comings: in the past, in the present, and in the future. The Advent wreath with four blue candles representing the four weeks of Advent is a symbol of victory and glory that is the fulfillment of time in his eternal comings.

To help us celebrate this season appropriately, we typically hold both a service of lessons and carols during Advent and later during Christmastide (the twelve days of Christmas) to remind us of the significance and relatedness of the two seasons.

Christmas

Christmas is not a season of nostalgia and escape from the harsh realities of life, but rather of a time of awareness of God's promise of new possibilities amidst what may appear to be an impossible situation. It is a time to remember how God entered into human life and history as a child, thereby blessing the material world and our life in it. It is a time to remember how God continues to do so. Christmas is the mystery of possibilities, the mystery of the saving action of God in our lives and history. It is an action that appears as a child, innocent and powerless. It is best understood in terms of John's image of a candle in the dark, a flickering light that makes it possible for us to see the outlines of new possibilities in the midst of our darkness (John 1:3–9). It is the story of how that flickering light can never be put out, but will always provide us with enough light to walk into the night. Christmas is that season in which we are reminded that, in spite of all evidence to the contrary, the promise of Good Friday and Easter will be realized, but that God's means for doing so will always be found in the mystery of a child and the birthing of new possibilities.

Epiphany

On Christmas we celebrate the birth of the human Jesus. On Epiphany we celebrate the manifestation of the divine Christ. God's manifestation in Jesus in the Western church was connected with the story of the adoration of the magi. The baptism of Christ and the miracle of Cana were also commemorated during this season of epiphanies or revelations. A revelation is first an act of God, but it does not become a revelation until we respond. Therefore, the feast of the Epiphany celebrates our going to God.

Epiphany is a season for dreamers, for people who see visions, hear voices, follow stars, and live naïvely. Who but imaginative, naïve, childlike persons and mad magicians might imagine, let alone go in search of a child who, on love alone, will build his kingdom, whose pierced hands will hold no scepter, whose hallowed head will wear no crown, whose might will not be built on military, economic, or political power, who will receive our deaths and bring us new life. Epiphany is the story of a childlike visionary quest, a pilgrimage of all those who are aware that their calling is to abide in God's reign and thereby join God in God's continuing action.

The biblical story of the magi (the illustrious ones) was enhanced over time. For example, St. Bede the Venerable in the eight century wrote that there were three magi. The first was Melchior, an old man with a white beard who brought an offering of gold to Jesus, his earthly king. The second was Gasper, a young, beardless man who brought incense, an act of homage to announce Christ's divinity. And the third was Balthazar, a man of dark complexion who brought myrrh, a gift that prefigured Christ's suffering and death.

Over time, Epiphany became a season to remember the mission of the church to proclaim the gospel, to trust in God, and to live as if God's reign has come, in spite of all evidence to the contrary. Epiphany is an invitation to go on a journey we cannot order or control, following in a way we cannot fully comprehend and the world deems foolish and irresponsible.

It is also a time to bless the homes of Christians with holy water, incense, and prayers, that those who abide in the home may be empowered to live lives that are an epiphany of God's coming among us in Jesus, into whose body we have been incorporated at our baptism.

Lent

There is a time in the story of our pilgrimage when we become aware of lost innocence. The naïveté of childhood ends and we face the hard realities about ourselves, others, and the world. Lent is the season of adolescence. Having attempted to live as childlike dreamers, we turn to reflect on what we have done. It is the story of the adolescent struggle for identity and purpose. Once again we become aware of the principalities and powers. We become aware of evil and the temptations that surround us. We become aware of how we have denied and distorted the truth about ourselves.

Lent, like every season, is lived in the light of Good Friday and Easter. But just as in every Advent we open ourselves to being pregnant with God, every Christmas we give birth to a new possibility, and every Epiphany we live in the naïveté of childlike dreams, every Lent we face up to the struggle to acknowledge who and whose we really are and to the continuous battle with the principalities and powers that work against our actualizing our true identity. Lent is that serious penitential season when we prepare for the reaffirmation of our baptismal vows and covenant.

Lent begins on Ash Wednesday. Shrove Tuesday precedes it. Shrove Tuesday was the day when the people were shriven from their sins. They participated in both the rite of recollection, known then as confession, and a carnival day of drinking and feasting in preparation for a season of fasting, which concluded with the symbolic burial of the word "Alleluia" (the praise of the Lord), to be resurrected on Easter day.

Ash Wednesday marks the beginning of Lent, a season of forty days during which we are to participate in a prayerful and penitential preparation for the great feast of Easter. Lent is marked by the liturgical color purple, suspension of the words "Alleluia" and "Gloria," and the prohibition of weddings and other joyous celebrations except burial services, which are resurrection rituals. On Ash Wednesday, we participate in a ceremony of imposing blessed ashes made from the palms of the previous Palm Sunday liturgy in the form of a cross on the foreheads of the faithful. They are reminded, "from dust we have come and to dust we shall return," that is, we are reminded of our humanity and of our absolute dependence upon God.

Lent is marked by self-examination and repentance culminating in the Rite of Reconciliation; by prayer and meditating on Holy Scripture; by fasting (not eating between sunrise and sunset on Fridays to remind us what food we need most for life); and by acts of self-denial, best understood as acts or positive practices that enhance an ever-growing and loving relationship with God, such as being more generous to the poor and caring for the homeless. But the main emphasis is on preparation for the renewal of our baptismal vows and covenant at the Easter vigil.

And so the church year begins once again. Our storybook calendar is ready to repeat itself. We are invited once again to participate in that lifetime pilgrimage of making God's story our story.

However, if we are to be a faithful pilgrim people, we need to do more than participate in an experience of our story through worship. We will need to take that story and let it inform our lives at home and at church.

For example, Advent is intended to remind us that while both contemplative and active life are the two dimensions of faithful life, the contemplative life is to come first. Similarly, while the spiritual life is related to and must be manifested in the moral life, the spiritual life precedes the moral life. In a world in which we are defined by what we do and not who we are, taking time to be is depreciated. Still, Advent is intended to encourage us to take time to be contemplative and to practice living between the times, between the already and the not yet of God's reign, between Christ's first coming long ago and Christ's second coming when God's promises are fulfilled. This would require that we slow down and eliminate as much activity as possible in our homes and churches for these four weeks. It would mean putting off holding Christmas parties and the like until the twelve days of Christmas—or even the season of Epiphany. Of course, this would be extremely difficult in our secular society, but at least we might practice it in church and in our own homes.

And then, during the great fifty days of Epiphany, we need to turn to doing—not just any doing, but doing that witnesses to the gospel.

It is a season for families and the church to focus on the mission of the church and our baptismal promises to "seek and serve Christ in all people, loving our neighbor as ourselves" and "to strive for justice and peace, respecting the dignity of all people."

Every church and home will manifest our Christian story differently during the seasons of the church year. What is important is that we imaginatively explore and plan for ways that permit God's story to dominate, direct, and control how we live.

For too long we have been willing to live in goal-oriented, task-oriented religious institutions organized around a host of unrelated committees and programs in areas such as education, parish life, outreach, worship, and the like. What might it mean if we set out to be a people committed to live together as a story-formed community of faith so that we might become the body of Christ, Christ's presence and action in the world, to the end that all people might be restored to unity with God and with each other. Perhaps we can imagine a vestry that oversees a series of committees, one for each season of the year, which would prayerfully reflect on God's story as it might be lived out in every aspect of the lives of the people at church and at home. And then, based on these reflections, plan, design, and execute programs and resources for an intentional, integrated life as a pilgrim people.

CHAPTER 5
LIVING AS A PRAYERFUL PEOPLE

The spiritual life is best understood as ordinary, everyday life lived in an ever-deepening and loving relationship with God. Indeed, that relationship is our common human vocation or calling. Planted within the human spirit, therefore, is a restlessness and longing for unity with God. This unity is the very meaning and purpose of human life. The providence of God is the assurance that nothing and no one can prevent us from fulfilling this meaning and purpose. God's greatest desire and will is to do everything to actualize this relationship. And only our will can prevent it. The moral life is ordinary, everyday life lived in an ever-deepening and loving relationship with our true selves (the self that is the image and likeness of God), with all other selves, and with nature. It is the spiritual contemplative life that makes the moral active life possible. At the same time, the moral life is the test of the spiritual life. We cannot be growing in our relationship with God if our relationships with our neighbors are not becoming more loving, peaceful, and just.

Prayer is anything we do to enhance, enliven, support, sustain, or help this twofold relationship. Prayer, therefore, is both cultic life and daily life.

Theological Reflections on Prayer

There are those who believe that God exists outside the natural order but can and will intervene directly into human affairs and even alter the laws of nature, acts of God that are understood to be miraculous. Prayer in this case is our human attempt to influence or persuade God to act in particular ways. Having convinced God to act, these people can trustfully sit back and wait for God to do so. Such folk believe that God has unlimited power to do anything God wishes. Indeed, for them, God is in absolute and total control of every aspect of human life and history. For example, God is the cause of their diseases, which are intended to serve some purpose in God's plan such as punishing their sins or testing their faith. God can also cure their diseases if they ask forgiveness for their sins, have faith in God's power, and are persistent in their prayers. And if their prayers are not literally answered, they conclude that there must be something wrong with them, their prayers, or their faith.

Others believe that God exists outside the natural order but cannot and will not intervene directly in human affairs or alter natural law. For them, there are no miracles. From their perspective, God is not the cause of diseases, nor does God cure them. God created the world, established the laws of nature, and turned this world over to our keeping. Prayer, therefore, can affect the one who prays, but not God. These people pray so that they can discern what God wills for them to do. Through their prayers they may also be empowered to act or be aided to live with what fate and the acts of others deliver to them.

My own convictions are quite different from either of these positions. I believe that God is present and active both in- and outside of every human life. God is the innermost heart of reality, but God has placed a number of limits on God's self. First, so that we can live in relationship with God, God has granted us total freedom. Therefore, unless we acknowledge our dependence on God and seek to do God's will, God can do nothing for us. Further, God has chosen to be fully dependent on us. Therefore, God can accomplish nothing unless we cooperate with God. Our relationship is intended to be interdependent and mutual. Prayer is the necessary condition God has established for our life together. Prayer, therefore, affects both us and God. So from this perspective, there are miracles in the sense that we are able to recognize and acknowledge this cooperative effort and its effects.

God has a will for us and God has the power to help us actualize God's will, but not without our willingness and help. God does not need to be begged. And God cannot be manipulated. God only requires that we identify what God is striving to do with and for us and thereby discover what we need to do with God. Prayer is, therefore, not talking to God, but cooperating with God.

Have you ever heard someone pray, "God be with us" or something to that effect? Theologically, that is not the issue. We do not need to invite God into our lives. God is already present. This issue is, are we aware of God's presence? Perhaps it would be more faithful to pray, "Ever-present God make us aware of your presence, enable us to hear your word, but let none of our words go unjudged by your redeeming spirit."

Have you ever considered praying for a parking space? Would such a prayer be moral? What if God answered your prayer and someone who might need it more would be denied the space? A more moral prayer might go like this: "O God of all people, your justice is giving us all what we need most, so answer my desire for a parking place with what I need most, a lessening of my anxiety."

Jeremy Taylor was a seventeenth-century Anglican divine who wrote a book entitled *Holy Living*. In it, he counseled us to care about time. By this he meant: Begin and end each day in prayer, focusing our attention on our relationship with God. Using spare moments to say to God: I love you because _____. I am grateful to you for _____, I am sorry about _____, I offer to you _____, I intercede for _____. I desire _____. Taylor advised us that holy living requires the keeping of a Sabbath, that is, taking leisure seriously. While work is done for some other end, leisure is its own end. It is time to be rather than to do. We also need to take holidays (holy days) rather than vacations or escape time. Reading and meditating on spiritual literature and books on the life of prayer are also important.

Taylor also spoke about doing all that we do to the glory of God. This implies having only one end for life, our relationship to God, and making everything else a means toward that end. It implies making sure that our motives are as pure as our actions. It implies practicing a virtuous life by asking God's help in all we do. It means desiring only the approval of God and never separating our private and public lives. It also means not being attached to anything material and not worrying about outcomes, such as making a difference or being successful, but only striving to be faithful.

Taylor then talked about practicing the presence of God, that is, striving to be ever more conscious of God's presence and action in human life and history. We need to look for things for which to be thankful, live with moderation, and learn to float, that is, to cooperate with God. We must not compare ourselves with others but seek to develop our own personal spiritual discipline. And finally, we should devote our lives to acts of charity. That is all good advice, and the daily offices in the Book of Common Prayer are intended to aid us to live such a holy life.

Communal Prayer

We cannot underestimate the importance and value of communal prayer. In private prayer we have a tendency to focus on petitions concerning our needs, wishes, and concerns and sometimes those of others. In contrast, in communal prayer we are encouraged to offer our praise, adoration, and thanksgiving. Remember that the English word "worship" come from the Anglo-Saxon "worthship," the giving of honor and blessing to the one who possesses true worth. Communal prayer is the church's public testimony to God's incomparable truth, goodness, and the beauty of God's holiness.

When the daily offices were inserted into the Prayer Book, two traditions were merged. One was the Benedictine monastic tradition in which everyone participated and the liturgy was led by a layperson. Numerous psalms were sung seated in a stark contemplative environment, the scriptures were read and "prayed," and prayers were prayed together. There was no sermon. The other was the cathedral tradition, a more elaborate rite led by clergy and choir. The congregation was passive. They were observing participants praying privately in the presence of a cathedral choir. Because the choir was singing psalms focused on praise and intercession for the congregation, the choir members stood. Typically, at the close of this rite, a priest delivered an instructional or expository sermon to the congregation.

Regretfully, these two traditions were never satisfactorily united and over time what was intended to be communal prayer became private devotion and communal worship became a weekly rather than a daily event.

There is, however, another way to think about these two traditions of prayer, a way that might more easily unite them and help us reform our daily life of common prayer. The first image is that of "city prayers," which engage us with the world and incorporate the world into our prayers. These prayers are communal and embodied. Meditation engaging the senses plays a role and the sacrifice of praise and thanksgiving on behalf of all creation is articulated in hymns and psalms. The second is "desert prayer," which withdraws us from the world. Prayer is more personal, inward looking, and contemplative, and its aim is to sanctify the prayer's life. Silence and centering that disengages the senses, contemplative presence, and listening dominate. These two ways of praying can and need to be affirmed when we think about praying the daily offices and can be integrated into the daily office.

Regretfully, however, it is not clear that we who are the church either see a need for the daily offices or are willing to make a place for them in our busy lives. My experience is that even clergy who participated daily in a spiritual discipline that included participation in the daily offices while in seminary abandon these practices after graduation.

The provision in the Prayer Book of "Daily Devotions for Individuals and Families" is an attempt to help busy people build prayer into their daily lives, but in my experience, it has not been too successful. Further, in a land where individualism is a way of life, few who read the offices personally and privately have any sense of being part of a great worldwide community at prayer.

Contemporary life in our privatized, activist, work-oriented culture will, I suspect, find it difficult to reinstitute the daily offices. Personally, that makes me sad. For a significant time in my life I lived in community with members of the Society of St. John the Evangelist (one of our vibrant male monastic communities) in their house in Durham, North Carolina, near the campus of Duke University. Entering into their common life and participating in the daily prayer transformed my spiritual life, and I will always be grateful for that experience. Since then, I have tried to bring clergy and laity together for at least one daily office a day, but I have been unsuccessful.

But I have not given up. Perhaps we can imagine and design a contemporary evening prayer liturgy combining both "city and desert" ways of praying for Sundays or some other day of the week that might include an instructional sermon aimed at helping us all learn to interpret scripture and to think theologically faithfully in our day.

And there are other things we can try; for example, we can take every opportunity to go on short retreats and/or participate in the liturgical life of a monastic or semi-monastic community. Second, we can strive to organize a small group of people in our congregations, even if that means only two people at any one time, who perhaps with other small groups might take turns praying morning, noon, or evening prayer together, even if only once every two weeks or so. Third, we can suggest a weekly or monthly celebration of Evensong in our congregations with an instructional expository sermon on scripture as a means of improving adult education in the context of prayer. Fourth, we can encourage those attending meetings or some event at church to incorporate an appropriate daily office, perhaps Compline, at the end of their event or meeting. Fifth, we can use the "Order for Evening," with its lighting of candles before the evening meal, on Friday or on some other night each week before supper. And we can also build a spiritual discipline through personal prayer.

Personal Prayer

As you consider these various ways to pray, you may seek out a spiritual director to encourage and help you. To enhance and enliven your understandings of prayer, try some of the following.

Praying the Psalms

The Book of Psalms is found in the third section of the Tanak (the Jewish Bible). The psalms are not sacred history or teachings of the faith as found in the Torah, the five books of Moses. Nor are they divine revelation as found in the Prophets. Rather, they are part of the wisdom tradition, which makes discoveries about the nature and character of God by reflecting on experience. As such, they provide us with three orientations. First, there are prayers that express our experience of the ordered, reliable, life-giving world God intends. Second, there are prayers that express injustice, estrangement, our experiences of the absence of God, and our cries in the night for justice and peace. And third, there are prayers that express thanksgiving and praise for God who redeems and surprise us with new life amidst our experience of death. Walter Brueggeman refers to them as psalms of orientation, psalms of disorientation, and psalms of new orientation.[1]

The psalms are liturgical prayers and blessings written over many centuries by numerous authors. They represent the whole range of human experience with God. They vividly present the perennial dialogue between God and humanity through poetic imagery. They speak to our spiritual quest for wholeness and health in terms of unity with God, engaging both the full range of human emotions and the living presence of God.

The psalms take various forms. There are psalms of praise and thanksgiving; psalms of trust in God and hope for the future; psalms of sorrow and complaint by both individuals and the community; psalms concerning the leaders of the community; psalms about the wisdom that results from reflection on experience; and psalms that are intended for worship in the temple.

The psalms are a rich source for our thinking about God, for as the old saying goes, *lex oradni, lex credendi,* the rule of prayer is the rule of faith. The psalms explore questions about creation and redemption; the salvation history of the community; the roles and functions of their anointed leader; the interpretation of the Torah or teachings of the community; the wisdom gained by reflection on experience; and questions about violence, suffering, and death.

However, the Book of Psalms is not only a collection of prayers and blessings, but a school for prayer. As such, they teach about how we are to relate to the reality of God's presence and action in human life and history; they teach us the importance of praying out of our community's experience, history, and tradition; they teach us that the heart of prayer is to be found in the intuitive way of knowing and thinking, that is, through imagination and imagery; and they teach us that while prayer is an intensely personal matter, it needs to involve not only our whole self, but all of life and our community's experience. In praying the psalms, our aim is not to understand the world in which they were written or the faith of those who wrote them. Rather, we pray them to discover the light and wisdom they can shed on our lives. While each of us brings his or her own history and personal experiences to the reading of the psalms, no other book in the Bible speaks more helpfully to our spiritual quest: our desire to find God and our frustration with the fact that God seems remote, unapproachable, and unknowable. The psalms speak of human pain and suffering, human fear and despair, and our experience of being abandoned by God. They speak of our personal failures and the distrust of being betrayed by those we trusted. They identify with and express every possible human emotion and therefore can bring us into an ever-deepening and loving relationship with God. We read and pray the psalms because they bring our lives and God's grace together.

If you are praying the psalms alone, there are a number of possibilities. First, read the psalm prayerfully and pull out one phrase that speaks to you and simply repeat it over and over again with your breathing. For example, when I was reading Psalm 62, I came upon the phrase "For God alone my soul in silence waits" (vv. 1 and 6) and I turned it into the prayer "For you alone my soul in silence waits." As a second example, consider prayerfully reading Psalm 137. In this song of lament the psalmist is longing to return to Jerusalem but is prevented from doing so by the Edomites. In anger and frustration, he asks God to take the children and dash their heads against a rock. (I suspect the psalmist never believed God would do such a thing, but it surely made him feel better to say it.) Now personalize this psalm so that you can pray it faithfully.

For example, first ask yourself what you are longing for and what either inside you or outside you is getting in the way of your longing. And then express your honest feelings to God. Now turn your reflections on this experience into a prayer and be silent so that you might hear God's response.

Or third, take a psalm and read it phrase by phrase, turning each phrase into a personal statement. For example, Psalm 90:1, "Lord you have been our refuge from one generation to another," might become "God you have mysteriously always been there for me and my family when we needed you most" (v. 4). "For a thousand years in your sight are like yesterday when it is passed" might become "Your understanding of time is so different than mine and that limits me" (v. 12). "So teach us to number our days that we may apply our hearts to wisdom" might become "Help me to remember that I was born to die." Verse 14, "Satisfy us by your loving-kindness in the morning; so shall we rejoice and be glad all the days of our life," might become "Help me to know that there is only one end for my life, namely, to grow in an ever-deepening and loving relationship with you and if I pursue that end my life will have meaning and purpose now and forever."

Praying Scripture

While the study of scripture is essential to a faithful life, it also has limited value. When we study the scriptures, we turn them into an object for our investigation. When we pray the scriptures, we turn them into a subject that engages us. The spiritual reading of scripture is different than an academic reading. Both are important, but in praying scripture we must engage our imaginations, while in studying scripture we must engage our intellects. In praying scripture, we involve ourselves subjectively; in studying, we investigate it objectively. In praying the scripture we dwell with the text, while in studying it we reflect upon the text. And in praying scripture we strive to relate to our lives, while in studying it we dissect the text to better comprehend its historical meaning.

In the tradition of the church, the praying of scripture was known as *lectio divina*. This process of divine reading of scripture has been described in various ways; here is mine:

Lectio (to read). If a lesson is read in public, it should be read very slowly and clearly so that the listeners can fully hear it. If you read it alone, you may want to read it more than once aloud until you have made it your own.

Meditatio (to meditate). Enter the passage fully. Be present to it, enter into it, and let it engage you completely and personally. Exercise your imagination and experience the text.

Oratio (to pray). Converse with God about your experience. That is, reflect on your experience with this piece of scripture until God reveals to you some insights and implications for your life of faith.

Contemplatio (to contemplate). Be silent before God, empty your conscious mind, and open yourself to receive the grace God desires to give you so that you might, with God's help, live out the implications of your conversation with God.

As an example, read Mark 10:46 ff. It is the story of Bartimaus the blind beggar. As I once read this story, I became aware that it was for me more about spiritual blindness than physical blindness, and that there were aspects about my life about which I was spiritually blind. I entered into that experience and heard Jesus' question: "Do you want to be healed?" Following my immediate response, "Of course," I had to face the problem that if I were healed, my whole life would need to change. Like Bartimaus, who no longer could support himself by living off those who contributed to his situation and who would need to get a job and support himself, so I had to face the cost of God's healing of my blindness and decide if I really wanted to be healed or not. Moreover, if I accepted healing, I wondered what gifts and graces I would need and what I would need to do to open myself to receive these gifts.

Centering Prayer

Nothing is more important or more difficult than that contemplative silence which can lead us into an experience of unity with God, a unity in which we not only experience God's presence but also "hear God's voice." Praying short prayers we know by heart and repeating phrases that speak to our deepest desires over and over again with our breathing can help us to keep our conscious, busy mind occupied so that our unconscious might dwell with God. In our busy, noise-filled world, nothing is more important than centering prayer, prayer that can provide a means to achieve interior silence.

As an example, consider one of my favorites. It is the phrase "Gentle, loving God, the mother of my soul, hold me as your own." Sitting quietly with my eyes shut, I repeat this phrase over and over again in a rhythm with my breathing until I enter a state of feeling embraced by God's love. I then stop repeating the phrase and bathe in the grace of God's love. If I lose the feeling, I begin my mantra again.

Praying the Collects

A collect is a particular kind of prayer in which we collect or focus our minds, hearts, and wills on some aspect of our relationship with God. The aim is to make that focus a reality in our lives. Each is typically comprised of a number of parts: We address God, we name an attribute of God or one of God's saving acts. We make a request for something we already know that God desires for us. We state the reason for which we ask. And we conclude with a doxology.

The collects in our Prayer Book come from various sources and different times in history. They each have a biblical foundation and encompass some aspect of the Christian life of faith. Each is a theological statement worthy of meditation. Each also can help us learn to pray.

We can also write our own collects, but first we need to learn how to pray faithfully and morally by using the collects in the Prayer Book.

For example, we need to make sure that we name God in a faithful way. "Almighty God" is not the only or perhaps the best way. When most people think of God as powerful, they think in terms of might. However, the power of God—suffering love—is what the world calls weakness. Other options, therefore, are ever-present God, ever-loving God, ever-suffering God, and so on.

Study the collects in the Prayer Book to help you to understand how to pray faithfully and morally. For example, the collect "For rain" (p. 828), "O God our heavenly Father, who by your Son Jesus Christ has promised to all those who seek your kingdom and its righteousness all things necessary to sustain their life: Send us in this our time of need, such moderate rain and showers that we may receive the fruits of the earth. . . ." Please notice we did not ask for something we did not desire for everyone and we did not ask for sun so that we could have a good vacation or play golf. And then explore what other collects in the Prayer Book pray for, such as "our enemies."

When you are ready, begin to practice writing your own collects. Not only is the writing of the collect an experience of prayer, we can later enter into a deeper experience of prayer by repeating our own collects from memory. Here are three examples of collects I have written:

> O God of all who have known faith and doubt, deliver us from the desire for certainty; and grant us the grace to embrace openness and ambiguity while trusting that your Spirit will lead us into truth and fullness of life. Grant this for the sake of your love. Amen.

> O God of all who have known hope and despair, deliver us from the temptation to be a pessimist; and grant us the grace to embrace your redemptive presence in our lives, transforming sorrow into joy, brokenness into wholeness, death into life. And all for your love's sake. Amen.

> O God of all who have known love and hate, deliver us from the sin of indifference; and grant us the grace to never stop caring, while always tempering our anger with mercy so that we might be instruments of your reconciling love. Grant this for the honor of your name. Amen.

The Lord's Prayer

You may have noticed that the Lord's Prayer is placed just before we say our communal prayers in the daily office, but it is at the close of the eucharistic prayer in the Sunday liturgy. The reason is this: In the daily office its intent is to instruct, remind, and aid us to pray in terms of cultic prayer, while in the Eucharist it is to instruct, remind, and aid you to pray in terms of daily life

The model for all prayer is Jesus in Gethsemane. Jesus says, "God, what do you desire?" God responds. And Jesus confesses that he wished it were otherwise, but then says, "Your will be done." And it is. We often forget that prayer is the means by which we become aware of what God would like us to do together. And then we make the necessary response so that our prayer might be fulfilled. One way to view the prayer that Jesus taught his disciples is in terms of questions we are to bring to God so that we might learn God's will and with God's help, do it.

As a daily prayer, consider asking the following questions and responding positively to what God says to you or to your community: OUR FATHER IN HEAVEN: What do you want to make possible in my (our) life that neither I nor any other human being can make possible? HALLOWED BE YOUR NAME: What do you want to make whole and holy in my (our) life this day? YOUR KINGDOM COME: How can your reign of justice and peace come through me (us) this day? YOUR WILL BE DONE ON EARTH AS IN HEAVEN: What are my (our) Gethsemanes about which I need to say "your will be done"? GIVE US TODAY OUR DAILY BREAD: What nourishment do I (we) need most this day? FORGIVE US OUR SINS AS WE FORGIVE THOSE WHO SIN AGAINST US: For what do I (we) need most to be forgiven and with whom do I (we) need to be reconciled? SAVE US FROM THE TIME OF TRIAL AND DELIVER US FROM EVIL: From what do I (we) need to be protected?

The Apostles' Creed

Remember that the Apostles' Creed is your baptismal creed. Each day we need to remind ourselves who and whose we are. One custom is to take your thumb and make a cross on your forehead at the end of the creed just as you were signed with the cross and marked as Christ's own forever at your baptism. Also remember that the creed is a love song in which you give your love and loyalty to the triune God: God the Father, God the Son, God the Holy Spirit. Each day we can renew our love affair with God by prayerfully repeating the Apostles' Creed slowly and imaging each phrase.

Prayers of Disordered Affections

A disordered affection is nursed anger. Recall that Jesus said, "Do not be angry." However, in Greek there are two words for anger. One points to the anger that flares up and dissipates; the other, the anger that smolders and builds up. It is the latter that Jesus condemns. There is nothing wrong with being angry and expressing it, but nursing anger is spiritually destructive and eventually will lead to violence against one's self or another. Prayers of disordered affections are intended to deal with the anger that we are nursing.

This is how it goes: Take the person or group with whom you are angry before God and in your imagination say and do everything you are feeling, no matter how bad it might seem. Keep doing this until you are too tired and empty to continue. Ask God to fill that void within you with God's love. Repeat this prayer until you have no more anger to nurse. And thank God for God's help.

Conclusion

Remember that there are many ways to pray. The next two I find particularly helpful at the end of the day. In the examination of consciousness, we engage in a prayerful exercise intended to help us become increasingly conscious of God's grace, God's loving presence and action in our lives. We begin by reflecting on our day and where we experienced God's grace. We then relive that experience in our imagination. Next we reflect on our day and identify those moments when we did not experience God's grace. Then, asking God's help, we dwell on those moments until we become conscious of how God was present when we thought God absent. After asking God's forgiveness for being unconscious of grace, we ask God for all the blessing we will need so that we will not miss God's presence in our life another day.

Another is the examination of conscience. In this prayer exercise, we go back to a moment in our lives when we experienced wholeness and health and in our imagination bathe in that grace again. Then we identify an experience of brokenness and incompleteness so that we might through our imaginations experience God's healing power. Having experienced that healing, we need to ask God to reveal to us what new behaviors God is calling us to as a consequence of our healing. And then, having imagined living this new way of life with God's help, we need to express our gratitude for God grace in our life.

But never forget that prayer has two dimensions: devotional life and daily life. Jesus teaches that we should "pray without ceasing." Prayer in this case is an intentional life lived in a dependent relationship with God, ever striving to know and to do God's will. But prayer understood in this way requires taking time to deliberately focus our lives on God through devotional acts.

CHAPTER 6

LIVING INTO OUR BAPTISM

⟨⟨⟨⟩⟩⟩

The Baptismal Rite represents the most radical reform in the Book of Common Prayer 1979. Among the most significant changes was the moving of the rite for Holy Baptism from the first of the pastoral life-cycle rites to its own special place between the liturgies for the most holy days in the church year and the Holy Eucharist, thereby establishing that Baptism is a full and complete rite of Christian initiation for both children and adult believers rather than a rite of passage related to birth.

Holy Baptism is now to be understood as full initiation by water and the Holy Spirit into Christ's body, the church. The bond that God establishes in Baptism is indissoluble. We can reject and/or distort it, but we can never deny who and whose we are. It is God who is the prior actor in Baptism, an action to which we respond. This explains why a baptism can never be repeated. While we may break our covenant with God, God never breaks God's covenant with us. An appropriate and necessary response to being unfaithful to our baptismal vows and covenant, therefore, is to reaffirm them over and over again.

Baptism makes the baptized person "a" Christian; it tells us the truth about ourselves. But to become Christian, we need to spend the rest of our lives living into our baptism, becoming who we already are.

Baptism is intended to be a public act in the presence of a congregation. From a theological perspective, at Baptism parents give up their children for adoption, adoption into a new family, the church, that accepts them and promises to nurture them in their new life in Christ as well as support their parents and godparents in the keeping of their promises. We do this symbolically by giving each child a baptismal name, such as John Henry or Nancy Caroline, and a new surname, Christian. It is for this reason that in the community's intercessions we do not include the surnames of those who have been baptized, only their Christian names. It is, therefore, most appropriate to celebrate a baptism in the congregation in which the parents and child intend to. live and worship, rather than in a grandparent's church or in the church where one of the parents had been baptized. Further, Baptism ought never be a private family event; Baptism is intended to be a church event.

Symbolic Occasions for Baptism

In order to help us better understand Baptism, it is recommended that baptisms be celebrated on five special occasions. The first is the Easter Vigil. Here we are reminded that in Baptism we die to our old self and are reborn with Christ into a new self. This is symbolically made real through immersion (a growing tradition in the Episcopal Church, especially with adults), in which we experience being drowned and resurrected to new life.

A second is All Saints' Day when we are reminded that in Baptism we are washed clean of all that might separate us from God and made a holy people, that is, saints. Pouring water over the heads of those being baptized is a symbol of this truth.

The next occasion is Pentecost, when we remember that in Baptism we are infused with God's Holy Spirit and thereby empowered to live a new life in faith.

Then there is the Sunday after Epiphany, the baptism of our Lord, which reminds us that Baptism is every Christian's ordination to ministry; to represent Christ and his church; to bear witness to him wherever we may be; and, according to the gifts given us, to carry on Christ's work of reconciliation in the world.

And last is the visitation of the bishop, which reminds us that in Baptism we are incorporated into a new family, the universal family of all the baptized.

In a large parish, there may need to be other times for baptisms. One obvious choice would be the parish's patronal feast or the Feast of the Transfiguration, when we remember that God became human so that we might become divine, that is, reestablished in the image of God.

Besides water and oil, there are two other historic symbols related to Baptism. First, a baptismal candle is lit from the paschal candle so the person being baptism will remember his or her call to be a light to the world, a sign and witness to the coming reign of God. Second, a cockle shell, a symbol of pilgrimage, holds three drops of water to remind us that we have been baptized into a Trinitarian understanding of God and that we are on a pilgrimage to live into the reality of our baptism. Sometimes a shell, which is unique like a snowflake, is used to pour water over the baptismal candidate and then given to him or her along with the candle so that each year he or she might remember and celebrate the baptism.

To summarize, in Baptism we are incorporated into Christ's body, infused with Christ's character, and empowered to be Christ's reconciling presence in the world.

The Baptismal Rite in the Prayer Book calls for adults or older children to be baptized before infants, thereby demonstrating that believers' baptism (baptism of those who are able to speak for themselves and to profess their faith) is the norm or standard for Baptism and that infant baptism is the legitimate exception. This is a good example of our Anglican *via media,* the holding in tension of two understandings of Baptism, and an equal commitment to both infant and believers' baptism. Infant baptism reminds us that God's grace comes prior to our response; that the community's faith comes prior to our faith; that Baptism is something we need to grow into; and that faith is a gift. Believers' baptism, reminds us that Baptism is a sacrament and not magic (being baptized does not give us God's love but makes us aware of the love God has already given us); that Baptism calls for a moral response; that it is intended to be a mature act; and that faith is necessary if we are to be aware of what Baptism offers us so that we might benefit from it. Only by holding these two understandings in tension can we hope to shape faithful people. If we celebrated only believers' baptism, we might come to the erroneous conclusion that we earn God's love by our faith and life. Similarly, a celebration of infant baptism alone could lead us into the error of believing there is nothing we need to do in response to God's unmerited, unconditional, unending love. Remember, God's grace is free, but not cheap.

Regardless of whether we are baptized as children or as adults, sponsors are necessary—the sponsors for children being both the parents and chosen godparents. Sponsors for infants make promises in their name and take vows on their behalf. It is anticipated that parents and godparents will accompany them on their spiritual journey and, by prayer and example, prepare them for their Confirmation, their first public affirmation of their baptismal vows and covenant. It is essential that parents and godparents engage in serious preparation for these rites, for only persons who are on a faithful pilgrimage of living into their own baptism and who take seriously their need to renew their baptismal covenant along the way can faithfully participate in the baptism of an infant they love. Later I will suggest ways for parents and godparents to prepare for this role.

This necessary preparation of parents and godparents explains why there is a new rite for the birth or adoption of a child to be celebrated at the Sunday Eucharist shortly after the birth or adoption of a child. As was pointed out earlier, it is anticipated that parents and godparents will then ideally begin a process of preparing for the renewal of their own baptismal promises, an act that theologically and morally legitimizes the baptism of the infant.

The baptism of an adult or an older child also requires special preparation. Sponsors for adults and older children signify their endorsement of the candidates and their intention to accompany them in their baptismal preparation and to support them by prayers and example in their Christian life. These sponsors are named when an adult or older child ideally begins a year or more of preparation for Baptism. Sponsors for adults or older children assume the same responsibility as sponsors of children and therefore need to be among the most faithful in the parish so that they might perform this important task.

Baptismal Vows

The rite of Holy Baptism begins with the presentation of adults and older children by their sponsors who have accompanied them during their preparation to receive the sacrament of Baptism. It continues with an acknowledgment that those who are to be baptized seriously desire it.

Then infants and younger children are presented by their sponsors, parents, and godparents, who promise with God's help to take responsibility for bringing them up in the Christian faith and life. This represents a promise to participate with them in the life of a community of faith and to practice with them the Christian life of faith. It is also a promise to pray with them and for them as well as to be for them an example of the Christian life of faith, thereby assisting this child to live into his or her baptism until she or he is ready to make a mature public affirmation of his or her commitment to the responsibilities of the baptized. There is no more awesome responsibility one can assume, and it ought not to be entered into lightly or without serious preparation.

Immediately thereafter follows a series of vows or declarations in the form of three renunciations and three adherences that are foundational to the life of the baptized and indeed a necessary precondition before persons are able to enter into their baptismal covenant with God faithfully.

A renunciation is an action in which we separate ourselves from a former condition or state by giving up former perceptions and allegiances and accepting the gift of a new set of perceptions and allegiances. To put it in another way, if you are walking in one direction, you see reality from that perspective and act accordingly. But if you repent, that is, turn around and change the direction you are traveling, you see reality from a new perspective and behave accordingly. That is exactly what a person does when he or she makes these three renunciations and adherences.

Our first act is to renounce evil, that is, to acknowledge evil's influence on our lives and to make a formal declaration to refuse, with God's help, to follow, obey, or be influenced by evil. To renounce evil is also to assert that with God's help we will not permit ourselves to be victimized by our experience of evil—evil that, in this case, is the result of its influence on others whose resulting actions affect us.

To understand the church's understanding of evil is difficult. Despite all attempts to explain it, evil remains a mystery best understood as both an active power or influence that desires to estrange us from God, and the experience of an absence of a God-desired good by the actions of those who have succumbed to evil's influence.

The good news of the Christian faith is that the power of evil to corrupt or destroy us has itself been destroyed. Evil continues to exist; we experience its influence and suffer from its consequences, but it has no power to affect our lives that we do not grant it.

It is important to acknowledge that God does not will evil, but God does permit evil for a greater good. That good is our human free will, a freedom necessary if we are to experience healthy relationships between ourselves and God, between each other, and between ourselves and the rest of God's creation. These relationships are God's greatest desire and good. Evil would have us misuse or abuse this freedom and thereby disrupt or destroy these relationships.

Sins are actions we engage in that are against God's will, but sin is the disposition to act in ways that negatively affect the relationships God intends for us to have with God, ourselves, other persons, and creation. Sin is not so much concerned with determining what is right or wrong as it is with determining what kind of person we will become if we continue to act in some particular way.

The good news of the Christian faith is that God's redeeming power is ever present, making new life possible. However, if that truth is to operate in us, we in our freedom must renounce the power of evil in our lives.

In the Baptismal Rite, we renounce three distinct manifestations of evil: cosmic evil, systemic evil, and personal evil. The first renunciation is this: "Do you renounce Satan and all the spiritual forces of wickedness that rebel against God?" Cosmic evil would have us believe that we have the power to manage nature and history. We experience cosmic evil in the unmanageability of nature and history. We also experience cosmic evil in physical and mental disease and in natural disasters that cause suffering for those who are not responsible for them. We also experience cosmic evil as a consequence of the actions taken by those who believe they can control nature and history.

The second question concerning renunciation is this: "Do you renounce the evil powers of this world that corrupt and destroy the creatures of God?" Systemic evil would have us believe that we have the power to manage human affairs and the social systems we create. We experience systemic evil as the disordering of human affairs in the structures of society and human relationships. Racism, sexism, classism, nationalism, and militarism are all examples. So are the various social, political, and economic systems we create with good intentions but that result in depriving some person or group of a good that God intends for them.

And the last question concerning renunciation is this: "Do you renounce all sinful desires that draw you from the love of God?" Personal evil would have us believe that we have the power to manage our own lives. We experience the consequences of personal evil when we are influenced by the historic dispositions to sin: pride, envy, nursed anger, sloth, greed, gluttony, and lust, as well as the consequences of our many addictive behaviors, which are themselves expressions of the influence of personal evil.

So it is that we are called upon to acknowledge that our lives are unmanageable and that our desire to be independent, self-sufficient, self-disciplined, self-interested, and self-determined, to be effective, to make a difference, to be successful, to be in control—all values of our secular society that are at the heart of our common human sickness and ultimately the foundation for our destruction—need to be renounced.

In other words, we begin our baptismal vows by admitting that we are powerless over those human dispositions that are a consequence of original sin, a doctrine that acknowledges a contradiction between who we really are as God's creation and how in our freedom we choose to live. Although we are formed in the image of love, the image of God, our souls from the moment of birth are affected by other influences that present us with images for our lives that are less than divine, images of human life that would have us deny and distort our total dependence on God and influence us to desire and act as if we have power that belongs to God alone. Or, in the case of some, to believe that they have no control over their lives at all and are always victims of the past or the actions of others.

Having acknowledged our human condition and renounced evil, we turn to three adherences. Having turned away from and rejected one way of life, we make a faithful attachment of our minds, hearts, and wills to an alternative way of life. That is what we mean by an adherence. Our first adherence is to the affirmation that there is a power greater than ourselves who can help us, namely, Jesus Christ, whom we, therefore, accept as our savior. He is the one who can save us, free us, liberate us from the influence of evil and our disposition to sin. To accept Jesus as our savior, of course, has a consequence that can be frightening. No longer can we blame our heredity or our environment for our human situation or attribute our behavior to the forces of evil in and around us. Now we must take responsibility for our lives. And depending on God to aid us, we can know and do the will of God, that is, live a faithful life.

Then, having affirmed Jesus' power to save us, we put our complete trust in his grace and love—we turn our wills and lives over to his care.

As dependent children, we surrender our lives to God; we allow God to be totally in charge of our lives. Having put our trust in God's redeeming or transforming power, we acknowledge that we are not alone. God is present and active in our lives and in history. We need never rely on our own strength and courage, our own wisdom and will. We need not act as if the primary aim for our lives is to be effective or to make a difference. We are to be concerned with being faithful, living in the difference God has already made, and doing God's will, always with God's aid. We do not need to build God's reign; we need only abide in it. And that means being willing to float.

Most people, in my experience, are not very good at floating. Perhaps it's true not because floating demands much skill, but because it demands much letting go. The secret to floating is in learning not to do all the things we are prone to do. It is not easy to relax, to give up control and float.

Typically, when people find themselves tossed from a boat at sea, they respond in one of two ways. Some panic and, being unable to swim, give up and drown. Others attempt to swim to safety. They too drown because they are setting their wills against the water's and the water's always wins. Only those who choose to float can survive. Now floating is not doing nothing. Floating is cooperating with the water. Still, all too few of us are willing to trust the water. Nevertheless, floating is our best analogue for the faithful life. It is neither striving to be in control nor permitting ourselves to be victims who are totally out of control. God calls us to discern what God is trying to do and to cooperate with God.

Having turned our wills and lives over to God's care, we promise to obey Jesus as the one who has legitimate power over our lives and to behave in ways that are a manifestation of Christ's character, that is, to live lives disposed to behave in ways that demonstrate what it means to be in the image and likeness of God. This implies making the character of Jesus the model for our lives and, therefore, apprenticing our lives to Jesus, that is, identifying with Jesus, observing his character or behavioral dispositions, and imitating them.

At this point in the rite, the congregation composed of recovering sinners—that is, saints who sin, who have witnessed these vows and who know that none of us can make them alone—promises to do all in its power to support those being baptized in their life of faith as members of the body of Christ.

The Baptismal Covenant

Having made these baptismal vows, we are prepared to enter or reenter into our covenant with God.

The frame of the creedal dimension of our covenant is "I believe in" and "Amen." The "I" is both personal and communal, in that while each of us must affirm our own faith, the faith we affirm belongs to the community. No one writes his or her own confession of faith; rather, we personally affirm the community's faith, its image of the nature and character of God, and God's promises to us. The "believe in" is not intended to be an intellectual acceptance of propositions concerning doctrinal truth. The phrase is rather an offering of our love, loyalty, devotion, and obedience to a particular image of God. It is an affirmation of faith. While faith can be used to indicate convictions, trust, or worship, faith is best understood as perception, that is, the way in which we see or image life and our lives.

Our underlying perception as Christians is that of a triune God: God the Father, God the Son, and God the Holy Spirit. Our God is a God who lives in and for community. To be created in the image and likeness of this God is to have been made for community, a community that comprises great diversity and yet has a common relationship with God. The "Amen" is our public profession that on this faith, this perception of life and our lives, we stake our lives.

By responding to three questions that are answered through a reaffirming of the sacred narrative that is the basis for our life together, we express our faith concerning the nature and character of the God who enters into covenant with us. This God is the one who creates, rules, and orders all life in sovereign, transcendent majesty, and yet who is a loving parent who nurses and nurtures us as sons and daughters. God longs for intimacy with us and for harmonious relations among all creatures and all creation. The world we inhabit belongs to this God, who has a purpose for all of creation and is present and active within it, acting to re-create and redeem all that we do to deny and distort that purpose. And in God's good time, God will, with our cooperation, bring creation and its creatures to their intended end.

This same God, we confess, entered human life and history in the person of Jesus of Nazareth to provide us with an image of who and whose we are and how we are to live. Jesus in his crucifixion joins us in our suffering and, through the power of suffering love, defeats the power of evil. In his resurrection and through the gift of the Holy Spirit, God makes it possible for us to become what God intends us to be: faithful brothers and sisters abiding together as a reconciled and reconciling people in God's reign, that is, a domination-free, nonviolent society of reconciled persons who live by the principle of justice as equity.

This God guides, goads, and strengthens us through the Holy Spirit as we endeavor to know and do God's will. God remains present and active in human life and history as Spirit, especially in the church, through which God is forever offering us reconciliation through the forgiveness of our sins, thereby enabling us to live into the truth of our baptism. This God can be trusted to see that nothing except our own wills can prevent us from fulfilling the meaning and purpose of our lives, that is, to grow into an ever-deepening and loving relationship with God for eternity. And this God is always redeeming our personal and corporate lives, turning negatives into positives, sorrow into joy, illness into health, death into life. Our life with this God of our faith is one of grateful response for all that God has done, is doing, and will do for us. And so we boldly make five promises, aware that God intends to provide us with the help necessary to make good on them.

We first acknowledge the need of life in a community of faith for formation, support, and encouragement; therefore, we promise to live into our baptism through study, personal prayer, and participation in the communal and sacramental life of a congregation.

Next, we acknowledge that while evil has no power over us, its influence surrounds us and without God's help we will surely succumb; therefore, we promise to live self-critical lives that are aware of sin and we commit to changing the direction of our lives continually so as to follow more closely in the way of Jesus.

Third, we acknowledge that we have an obligation to share with others what God has done for us and all people; therefore, we promise to live lives that are a sign and witness, in all that we say and do, to the good news of God's reign, that condition in which God's will is known and done.

We then acknowledge our gratitude for God's unconditional love, which has made a new way of life possible for all humanity; therefore, we promise to help those who reject or distort the truth about themselves to see that there is an alternative way to live by loving them as God has loved us.

5. And last, we acknowledge that God's reign of justice and peace, that is, of reconciliation, is a reality; therefore, we promise to demonstrate in gestures great and small what it means to live together as a people restored to unity with God and each other in Christ by committing ourselves to honor and respect the uniqueness and value of all people.

Baptismal Renewal and Preparation

But there is a difference between being "a" Christian and "being" Christian. When we are baptized we become "a" Christian, but to become Christian takes time and effort. We are always living into our baptism, that is, becoming who we already are. This is accomplished by God's action in our lives to which we respond positively. Therefore, it is expected that we will renew our baptismal covenant over and over again. The first time we do that is known as Confirmation. If a person has been baptized and has already made a public affirmation of faith, regardless of tradition, he or she renews his or her baptismal covenant upon being received into the Episcopal Church. Parents and godparents are reaffirming their baptismal covenant at their child's baptism. Others may choose to prepare for the reaffirmation of their baptismal covenant at some special transition in their lives, such as those life-cycle years of forty or fifty, before a marriage or after a divorce, upon a move to a new home, a change of parish, or a death. Further, to emphasize the need for renewal, it is expected that everyone in a congregation will renew his or her covenant on the various days set aside for baptisms, even if there is no one to baptize. And remember that Lent is the season for all Christians to prepare to renew their baptismal covenant each year at the Easter Vigil.

A healthy congregation provides the means to help us all to prepare for a meaningful reaffirmation of our baptismal vows and covenant. Such a process includes two dimensions: formation—an intentional practice of and participation in the Christian life of faith; and education—an intentional process of critical reflection on our lives in the light of the Christian life of faith, that is, on our baptismal vows and covenant.

Christianity is first and foremost a way of life resulting from a particular perception of God and human life that is faith. If we are to live into our baptism, we need to intentionally practice a way of life that includes communal worship, personal prayer, engagement with scripture, being good stewards of all our gifts and graces, practicing acts of love (personal and social) for all others in need, and serving God through our daily lives and work.

To prepare for the renewal of our baptismal vows and covenant, we need to take time to develop a plan for our continuing formation in the Christian life of faith and to reflect on our life experiences and actions as a baptized person. We will also need at least one other person with whom to share our experiences and reflections. Helpful suggestions are provided below, beginning with formational experiences.

Worship: a commitment to increase participation in the celebration of the Eucharist as well as daily morning and evening prayers with at least one other person.

Personal prayer: the development of a more intentional spiritual discipline of silence and solitude, daily devotions, the reading of spiritual classics, and a regular meeting with a spiritual director, confessor, or friend.

Scripture engagement: the establishment of a plan for a more serious reading, study, and meditation on scripture alone or in a group.

Christian service: a more healthy attendance to one's own personal needs and a greater acquaintance with and response to the needs of others, especially the poor, the hungry, the homeless, the sick, and the dying, and a commitment to address their needs by personal acts of caring and social acts of influencing public policy.

Stewardship: the development of a more disciplined life of being more a faithful steward of God's gifts to us and of God's creation. This would include increasing personal financial contributions to the church and to other needy causes, simplifying your lifestyle, increasing the use of your time and talent in the service of the needy, and engaging in practices that are ecologically sound.

Ministry within daily life and work: this implies being more intentional about understanding your daily life and work as the context for loving and serving God as well as practicing a way of life that manifests this understanding.

Having developed a personal formational program, we need to have at least one other person to help keep us accountable for our plan and with whom we can reflect on our actions and experiences and develop a more faithful life.

The second part of our preparation for the renewal of our baptismal vows and covenant involves critical reflection, a serious consideration of the meaning of these promises, a reflection on how well we have been doing, and specific commitment to be more faithful.

Earlier we discussed a theological understanding of evil. Now is the time to reflect on how we have experienced natural (cosmic) evil, systemic evil, and personal evil in our lives, what it will mean and look like for us to renounce its influence in our lives, and what help we will need from the church if our renunciation is to be sustained.

Then, turning to the adherences in which we commit ourselves to a new way of life, we need to consider what it will cost us to turn to Jesus Christ and accept him as our savior, that is, to acknowledge that we are free to act as healthy, mature persons and we alone are responsible for our thoughts, feelings, and actions. Then consider what it will cost us to rely totally on God's grace and love and finally what it will cost us to follow and obey Jesus. Then, having counted the cost, we need to ask how our new willingness to be faithful in spite of the cost will manifest itself in our lives and determine what help we will need from the church if we are to be faithful to our new resolves.

Having reflected on our baptismal vows, we turn to our baptismal covenant first in terms of the Apostles' Creed, in which we express our love and loyalty to a particular image of God. One way to do that would be to draw one or more pictures to express your experience of the presence or absence of God during the past year. And then reflect on these pictures and complete the following sentences: My relationship to God is like _____. What do I need to do to improve my relationship with God? How can I begin to develop an ever-deepening and loving relationship with God?

Finally, we need to reflect on each of the promises in terms of the following questions: What have you done about this promise during the past six months? What concretely do you intend to do in the year to come? What will you need from God if you are to realize this promise?

Before you make a reaffirmation of your baptismal vows and covenant before God and the congregation, it may be helpful to go on a short retreat to pray about your preparation and then when you return meet with others who will be renewing their vows and covenant to share and reflect on your experiences. If you are the only one, find a few friends with whom you can share your experience and solicit their help in keeping your new resolves.

CHAPTER 7
LIVING A EUCHARISTIC LIFE

Baptism is the foundation of our identity as Episcopal Christians. The making of Eucharist is the consequent responsibility of the baptized so that they may be nurtured and nourished to live into the truth of their baptism.

Nevertheless, in spite of this historic theological/liturgical conviction, there is a growing conviction among some Episcopalians that everyone, baptized and unbaptized, should be publicly invited to participate in communion as an experience of the radical hospitality of Jesus. This is referred to as "open communion" and is a violation of the church's present canons, which require baptism for those who wish to commune.

The theological issue, however, is not about denying communion to some unbaptized person who shows up at the altar rail expecting to commune. It is about a public, unconditional invitation made to everyone present. Indeed, it is not about pastoral hospitality, it is about the sacramental relationship between Baptism and Eucharist. Together, Baptism and Eucharist testify to the nature of salvation as both the radical gift of grace and the radical call to the cost of discipleship. At Baptism we are incorporated into Christ's body and in the Eucharist we are nurtured and nourished to be Christ's body in the world. One sacrament without the other is a distortion of this theological conviction.[1]

When we gather each week to make Eucharist, we make present again God's sacrificial mercy and love and we respond by offering our souls (our bodies, minds, and spirits) as a loving sacrificial gift to God. Another way to explain it is to say that each week we set apart a sacred time to become aware of God's grace, God's presence and action in our lives and history, made known to us in Baptism. And in doing so there is a meeting, an encounter, an exchange that is life giving and life empowering. And then we are sent forth as a baptized people to witness to the gospel of God's radical action in human life and history.

Through our weekly participation in the Eucharist, we are reconstituted as Christ's body, made aware that we are infused with Christ's character, and empowered to be Christ's presence in the world. Each week we come to experience again life in God's reign, where all people are restored to unity with God and each other in Christ and where God's will is known and done, so that we can return to our daily lives and work as a sign and witness to God's reign.

Our Anglican spirituality underlies our celebration of the Eucharist. This spirituality gives a central place to scripture. We recognize that scripture is a divine gift to the church. It is God's Word, "that God inspired its human authors and God still speaks to us through it today" (Catechism, 1979 Book of Common Prayer, 853). Our spirituality depends on communal rituals, repetitive symbolic actions, words and deeds through which we express and manifest our interpretations of scripture. Our spirituality is incarnational or embodied. We engage all our senses in a weekly dinner party in the reign of God after which we are prepared to go forth to love and serve God in our daily lives and work. We understand the Eucharist to be a sacrament, an outward and visible sign of an inward and spiritual grace. It is an action that both makes us aware of and makes present once again God's loving presence and action in our lives. Our spirituality tends to be mystical, that is, it emphasizes a lifelong pilgrimage of growing into an ever-deepening and loving relationship with God. And it is pastoral in that each week we bring our lives in their brokenness and incompleteness as a sacrifice, holy and acceptable to God, so that God may take our lives and transform them and give them back to us made whole.

Three gifts are granted to us through our participation in the Eucharist. They are faith, hope, and love. Faith is best understood as perception, how we image God, life, and our lives. Faith includes a vision of the future we desire, anticipate, and commit our lives to. The opposite of faith is not doubt. It is certainty. The desire for certainty is therefore a denial of faith. Hope is the assurance that God is present in human life and history. We are not alone and with God all things are possible. The opposite of hope is not despair. It is pessimism. And love is the experience of God's life-giving, life-transforming action in our lives that makes it possible for us to be a reconciled and reconciling community, a sign and witness to the reign of God. The opposite of love is not anger at injustice to be tempered by mercy. It is indifference.

Our lives as members of Christ's body are founded upon our experience of God's future, a future that is made present and actual for us during our participation in the Eucharist. At every Eucharist, we, the church, make present again that which happened long ago, and at the same time, make present now that which is yet to come in God's good time. Each week we come to participate in this banquet in the reign of God and experience the future God intends. This reign of God is that state or condition in which all people live together with God in a domination-free, reconciled, and nonviolent relationship in which everyone has all they need but no more than they need. This reign of God has arrived, but it has not yet come in its fullness. The reign of God is a vision of that reality that stands beyond, behind and within the passing flux of immediate things. It is real and yet waits to be realized, a reality that is in the future and yet present now. And we are called to abide in this reign of God's, that is, to live as if it has come, both until and so that it might come in its fullness. One way we do that is to share in the eucharistic feast. Baptism is the ritual commitment to life in the reign of God and Eucharist is the ritual remembrance in which this commitment is enhanced and enlivened.

Every Sunday God invites us to leave our homes, labors, and absorption in this world so that we might experience ascending out of "this world" to be participants in "the world to come." For a few brief moments we enter into a redeemed world, freed from the horrors of life in ordinary time and space. Miraculously, this is not an "other" world entirely different from the world of our daily lives and work. It is the same world, already perfected in Christ, but not yet perfected in us. It is the same old world we know best, but redeemed and restored in Christ.

Of course, this act of making Eucharist involves a costly giving, the giving up of our attempts to image God in our likeness and to recommit ourselves to see life and our lives through the eyes of God. Only then will we be enabled to put aside our preoccupation with life in this present world and to abandon our self-confidence in our abilities make this into a world worth living in. Only then will we be able to give up our false perceptions that we can and therefore ought to manage history and nature, our political, economic, and social systems, and our own lives. As we offer the sacrifice of our lives at this holy meal, we are acknowledging that the future is not something we can determine, construct, or control. We can accomplish nothing of value in this world without God's help. And God has chosen to accomplish nothing without our cooperation. And the gift of God's love is all we need to love ourselves, all other people, and God's creation. It is the experience of God's unending, unconditional, unmerited, reconciling love that empowers us to be a community of love.

Further, the church is shaped by the way it celebrates the Eucharist. Our Prayer Book contains "An Order for Celebrating the Holy Eucharist." We'll look at this structure next.

Gather in the Lord's Name

The people of God gather as a community of faith to draw near to God and to celebrate new life in Jesus Christ. From the birth of the church, the baptized have gathered to worship and serve the Father, to be nourished and nurtured by the Son, and to be equipped and empowered by the Holy Spirit. Community worship helps the baptized to be faithful witnesses to the gospel in daily life and work.

As part of this assembling, we need to take the time to disengage, to quiet our bodies, minds, and spirits, to open our lives to God's presence, and to prepare ourselves to participate fully in the Word of God and Holy Communion. To regress into a state of extra-dependence, that parent-child relationship with God which is necessary for us to experience the transforming love of God, is not easy in our busy, rushing, noisy lives. Unless the church offers us an environment conducive to this preparation, it will be difficult for us to fully benefit from our participation in the Eucharist.

In my experience, some worshippers come early, but mostly to socialize, sitting together and talking loudly to each other. Others arrive somewhat early and want to pray, but the talking and a loud organ voluntary make it difficult. But most arrive late, harried by the trip and still trying to catch their breath as the processional hymn begins.

All too often, the beginning of the liturgy is rushed. When that occurs, we have little time to establish an overall orientation toward God, to center ourselves and free our minds from distraction, and to focus on some particular aspect of our life of faith. This gathering, this collecting of the faithful, is a necessary reminder that we are called out of the world to be, by the mercy of God, the baptized daughters and sons of God among whom there is neither slave nor free, Jew nor Greek, male nor female.

My dream is that worshippers would come early enough to greet each other, welcome visitors, and catch up on their lives before entering the nave in silence. I have even thought that it would be helpful to begin a soft contemplative organ voluntary a few minutes after the hour the liturgy is scheduled to begin, to be followed by a few moments of silence before the processional hymn.

Proclaim and Respond to the Word of God

The scriptures are read and celebrated in silence and song, through meditation and preaching. A continuing conversation with the scriptures, especially with the gospels, is a necessary aspect of our life in the church, and Jesus promises that God will send "the Spirit of truth," the Holy Spirit, to guide the church in this never-ending task of interpretation (John 14:25–26).

Revelation is God's self-disclosure to individuals and communities. The scriptures are a record of that revelation. That is, they contain God's revelation, but they are not to be confused with the revelation itself. As the scriptures were written and edited over a long period of time, their human writers and editors were in conversation with earlier spoken traditions and written documents, quoting them, allegorizing them, correcting them, harmonizing them, interpreting and reinterpreting them, as well as adding new material. The scriptures as the church finally established them as canon—its measuring rod or standard for the Christian life of faith—are best understood as living, fluid records of the community's experience of God over time and therefore contain more possible meanings than their immediate and plain literal sense.

Because this was so, a host of methodologies for interpretation and schools of interpretation developed. For example, the New Testament became a commentary on Hebrew scripture. This in turn gave special authority to the gospels, which contain the narrative of Jesus' life, death, and resurrection and his teaching. And for some, John's gospel became normative for understanding the others. Have you ever noticed that in many churches the lectern from which scripture is read has an eagle, the symbol of St. John, prominently in front of it? Also, note how in the Eucharist we typically use a special gospel book that we carry in procession to give its reading special attention.

Nevertheless, our New Testament is filled with differing messages, conflicting stories, and various interpretations. While there is a unifying element in the scriptures, there is also substantial diversity of opinion. Each statement is culturally influenced, historically conditioned, and context specific. The scriptures are a literary, historical document written by human authors, a document in need of critical examination and interpretation.

As might be expected, controversies over interpretation developed even as the words were being written. The early church fathers established four means for interpreting scripture and made no attempt to harmonize them: 1) the *literal*, in which the meaning was self evident; 2) the *allegorical* sense, which taught about the church and its faith; 3) the *tropological* sense, which taught about persons and how they should live; and 4) the *anagogical* sense, which pointed to the future and awakened hope and expectation.[2] But in the church's search for unity and certainty, it chose to provide a way to establish a common interpretation of scripture. The Roman Catholic Church asserted that the church's authority was scripture and tradition, tradition being the interpretation of scripture established by the magisterium (the bishops). Indeed, this tradition was the only permitted interpretation and it was understood as unchanging. When the Protestant reformers established the scriptures as the only authority and returned their interpretation to the people, they had to find a solution to what they believed was the problem of numerous and different interpretations. They chose a means of interpretation that has made possible fundamentalism in our day, namely, the denial of any interpretation. The Bible says what it says. God wrote it and any who read it clearly will know and agree on what it says.

As Anglicans, we established a diffuse authority comprised of three interrelated, dependent authoritative sources: scripture, reason, and tradition united like three strands of rope.[3] Scripture is normative, but it does not have self-evident meaning as literalists would like to believe. Why? Because God communicated his revelation as contained in scripture in a manner sensitive to the specific needs of a specific group at a specific time in history, therefore intending that they be interpreted to make sense to a different people with different knowledge and experience in a different time. God's revelation was to be both inside and outside the scriptures, guarded and guided by the Holy Spirit.

This understanding is not unique. For many Jews there is a threefold Torah. The Torah represents the whole of Jewish teaching and is comprised of the "Written Torah" (the first five books of Moses), the "Oral Torah" (the tradition of interpretation passed down by word of mouth), and the "Silent Torah" (the teaching that emerges from that deep spiritual quiet through which God speaks in the present). This Torah of silence does not add to or replace the Written or Oral Torah; it clarifies and reinterprets them. It strips them of their tribal fears and patriarchal phobias; it cleanses them of xenophobia, misogyny, legalism, literalism, and idolatry by revealing something new and bold.

One of our best examples of how these three function is found in the Book of Acts (10:1ff., 11:4ff., 15:7ff.). Here we find the story of the Jewish Christian Peter and the Gentile Cornelius who want to be baptized. According to both the Written and the Oral Torah, he would first need to be circumcised. One day when Peter is at prayer, in his solitude and silence he has a vision (a mystical day dream), and in the quiet he hears the voice of God calling him to a new understanding of the Torah's teaching. And so in time the Silent Torah reinterpreted the Written and the Oral Torah and became the teaching of the community. In this case, it meant that Gentiles need not be circumcised before being baptized.

I suggest that this is similar to our understanding of authority as scripture (Written Torah), reason (Silent Torah), and tradition (Oral Torah). Reason in this case means prayerful reflection on experience that makes possible new understandings of scripture and interpretations of tradition. For example, while racism and slavery were long defended by scripture and tradition, reason eventually made it possible to reject both.

Jewish fundamentalists who take the Written Torah literally make no place in their religious lives for the Silent Torah. Similarly, Christian fundamentalists make no place for reason. Still, reason or critical prayerful reflection is important for us. Theological reflection takes place where scripture and tradition intersect with culture, human experience, and new knowledge. Conservatives, in their desire for certainty, deny the place of experience and new knowledge. And liberals, in their quest for personal self-assurance, neglect the role of scripture and tradition. Historically, we Episcopalians at our best keep these two sources for truth in prayerful conversation.

For this reason, Anglican's traditionally have never held to a doctrine of biblical supremacy (no other source of knowledge has any validity), literal interpretation (every word is literally true), or verbal inerrancy (God wrote each and every word). Rather, we have supported all forms of biblical scholarship and accept both changing interpretations and diverse opinions. While holding the scriptures in high regard, we do not describe them as having ultimate authority in all matters (for example, we allow science to inform us as to how the world was created; the creation story answers why, not how). Nor do we assert that everything found within them is binding on us (for example, we do not follow the dietary laws of Hebrew scripture). Further, we do not believe that scripture provides specific, final judgments on every moral or theological issue or question (for example, the writers were unaware of the possibility of genetic manipulation and they misunderstood how babies are conceived).

Importantly, we have believed that the scriptures are to be taken as a whole. No one part of scripture is to be taken in isolation from the whole. Each is to be heard in relationship to other themes and passages. We are not legalists and therefore avoid proof-texting, that is, using single passages for theological or moral conclusions unless that reference summarizes the whole.

So it is that historically, Anglicans have contended that the scriptures were intended to be interpreted and reinterpreted over and over again in the light of culture, contemporary knowledge, and human experience, within a worshipping community open to the leading of God's Spirit into new truth. Further, while maintaining that the scriptures provide us with a unifying plumb line, we have been willing to live with diverse and changing understanding rather than infallible certainty and binding prescriptions for all time.

In order that the church's story of salvation and its implications for life are explored faithfully, the church has established a lectionary, a set of readings from the Hebrew scriptures, followed by a sung psalm, a passage from the New Testament, and one from the Gospels. Our lectionary is found in the Book Common Prayer, but we have recently authorized the use of a Revised Common Lectionary developed by the Roman Catholic Church and sixteen Protestant denominations, including the Episcopal Church.

A lection is a selected reading, a lector is a reader, and a lectern is the place from which the reading is done. The lectionary is itself an interpretation of scripture based upon the liturgical year and a three-year cycle. Year A focuses on the Gospel of Matthew, year B on Mark, and year C on Luke. John is used on special occasions. During the first half of the year, from Advent to Pentecost, the readings focus on the story of salvation. The second half of the year focuses on its implications for our lives. Two other lessons and a psalm are established for each Sunday. The Hebrew scripture lesson in some way compliments the Gospel. The psalm is a commentary on the Hebrew scripture and the Epistle follows in course.

I would hope that worshippers would all prepare for Sunday by reading, studying, and prayerfully reflecting upon the Sunday lessons. Midweek Bible study groups devoted to this task could contribute much to more meaningful and purposeful worship.

Following the reading comes the sermon (from the Latin) or homily (from the Greek) for conversation. It is not intended to be an inspirational talk or entertainment. It is to be an exposition of the Gospel, a breaking open of God's Word so that God's people might be fed. That explains why the proclamation of the Word is also considered sacramental. A sermon is an oral interpretation of scripture for the life of a particular community in the context of the Eucharist.

The sermon can serve various functions: It can be a call to faith or to a deeper faith; it can provide instruction on Christian faith and practice; it can provide encouragement and comfort or other pastoral needs; it can strengthen our identity as Christians; it can reflect on our life experiences to help us grow in our relationship with God; it can provide a prophetic call to justice and peace; it can subvert how people see life and their lives so that they might see them through the eyes of God; or it can provide a bridge between the promises of the Gospel and the experience of Holy Communion.

R. Taylor Scott, who was on the staff of the College of Preachers at the Washington Cathedral, identities three "modes" for preaching based on three different understandings of preaching's purpose. The first mode is "rhapsodic." Focused on personal narrative, it intends to be uplifting and inspiring, to free us from the cares, troubles, and responsibilities of life, and provide us with an experience of rapture and peace. The opposite is a "rhetorical" mode. Its purpose is theological and ethical. Instructional and ideological in nature, it presents a rational apology and defense for the Christian life of faith. The third and preferred mode is "liturgical." Its purpose is to help us understand our life and work in the world as a holy activity, offered as an oblation, so that we might better serve God in the days ahead. Such sermons connect world and Word and unite word and sacrament. They begin with a conversation, a conversation with the Gospel, and lead us to a sacramental meal at which we will be granted the graces needed to manifest that Gospel in our daily lives and work.[4]

Because of its importance and significance in the lives of the faithful, preaching is limited to those who have been educated by the church in Bible, theology, church history, and ethics, namely, bishops, priests, and laypersons or deacons authorized by the bishop.

The response to this conversation on the Word of God is the Nicene Creed. No matter how much the sermon might have divided us, we are reunited as we pray this creed together. This creed begins: "We believe in," not "I believe." To believe in is to give our love and loyalty to the triune God revealed through the creed. The Christian faith is a way of life, more than the intellectual acceptance of particular doctrines or propositional truths. While this creed is the consequence of two ecumenical councils that met to address potential heresies and to establish orthodox interpretations of scripture, it was understood to be "a symbol of the faith," reflecting our image of the nature and character of God, the God we will meet in the Holy Eucharist. To emphasize this intuitive approach to the creed, it was often sung. What better response to the hearing of God's Word is there than singing a love song to God in thanksgiving for God's mighty acts on behalf of our and the world's salvation?

Pray for the World and the Church

These intercessions by the congregation are not merely another response to the ministry of the Word. They are better understood as an essential aspect of the priestly service of the body of Christ, the church. The symbol of the priest is to bring God to people and people to God, to intercede. Before the Reformation, the ordained priest prayed these prayers. The reformers established the concept of the priesthood of all believers. For many, this became the erroneous contention that each person was her/his own priest. Still, the pastor prayed the prayers. But that is a distortion. The priesthood belongs to all the baptized as a body, the body of Christ.

In the early church, those preparing to be baptized went through a lengthy period of preparation. They came weekly to participate in the first part of the liturgy, but then were dismissed after the sermon. During Holy Week, they were introduced to the contents of what would become the church's creed, to which they were to give assent at their baptism. Only then did they return to the assembled congregation to participate for the first time in the rest of the eucharistic liturgy. Significantly, the first thing they did was to pray the Prayers of the People. At Baptism they were told that they had been received into the household of God and were to confess the faith of Christ crucified, to proclaim his resurrection, and to share with all the baptized in Christ's eternal priesthood. They then acted accordingly. They joined in the priestly intercessions of the community.

Each Sunday we do the same. Led by a layperson to demonstrate the priesthood of all believers, we all intercede for the church universal, its members and its mission, the nations of the world and all in authority, the welfare of the world, the concerns of the local community, those who suffer and those in any trouble or need, and the departed.

These intercessions are to be written each week, making them relevant to the lessons so that they are a response to God's Word and relevant to the particular cultural, historical, and social situation. Six forms are provided as samples for various ways we can create these intercessions. My custom is to write the prayers of the people in relationship to the church year and to the life of my innercity parish. My hope is that as we pray them, we will be stimulated to ask how we might act as we cooperate with God in addressing the needs of our city.

But there always should be ways provided for every member of the congregation to express his or her own intercessions. Knowing how difficult it is for many to speak their concerns aloud, I know of a church that has an intercession sheet in the narthex so that people can write down intercessions that can be incorporated into the Prayers of the People.

The Prayer Book encourages us to write our own intercessions, intercessions that speak to the season of the year and the Gospel for the day. It is important, however, to include the following concerns: the universal church, its members and mission; the nation and all in authority; the welfare of the world; the concerns of the local community; those who suffer and those in any need or trouble; and the departed.

Here is an example of our Prayers of the People at St. Luke's in Atlanta for ordinary time (Sundays after Pentecost before Advent).

Jesus calls us to be his Body, his presence, in the heart of Atlanta; that we may have faith to live as Jesus lived, let us pray saying: *Send us your Spirit, Lord.*

You gave birth to your church that it might be a community of faith; that St. Luke's may always be a spiritual home for all people, let us pray together saying:

You gave us a vision of the city of God; that the leaders of every city, including Atlanta, may govern with justice and mercy, let us pray saying:

You gave your life for the sake of the whole world; that we may be empowered to give our lives on behalf of others, let us pray saying:

You bring the poor, the hungry, the homeless, the sick, the lonely, and the dying to our door; that we may lighten their load by sharing it with them. Let us pray saying:

You give us more than enough to share with the needy; that we may be dedicated always to be present to their needs, let us pray saying:

You have granted us the blessing of a park in the midst of this city; that it may always be a green space of peace and joy for all people, let us pray saying:

You taught us to pray for one another; that those who have asked for our prayers including (N) and others whom we now name (silent pause) that they may know your grace, let us pray saying:

You taught us always to give thanks. That we might be faithful to your teaching, we offer our thanksgivings for (insert) and we pray saying:

You have taught us to pray for those who have died, including (N); that they may know eternal life in your loving presence, we pray saying:

You have given us the Eucharist; that it might nourish and nurture us to be a sign and witness to the city of God in the city of Atlanta, let us pray saying: *Send us your Spirit, Lord.*

Throughout most of the year, following the Prayer of the People, there is a general confession. (During the season of Lent, we place the general confession within the context of a penitential rite at the beginning of the liturgy; during Eastertide, we eliminate the confession entirely.) Placing the confession after our intercessions helps us to understand that we as a community have a responsibility to connect the requests we address to God with our own behavior. For example, we pray for the poor, the hungry, the homeless, and the oppressed, but have we done everything we might do to meet their needs or are there things we have done that may have contributed to their situation?

Aware that we have already been forgiven, we confess our sins against God and our neighbor. Then, having experienced God's forgiving love, we accept the responsibility to make a new beginning. The general confession reminds us that, while we are justified by God's grace, that is, worthy to stand before the Lord, we are yet to be sanctified, to be made whole and holy. Therefore, both as a community and as individuals in a community, we are always in need of forgiveness for our sins

Exchange the Peace

Having been reconciled with God, we need to be reconciled with each other if we are to be who, by the grace of God, we really are—a reconciled and reconciling community that understands its mission to restore all people to unity with God and each other in Christ.

The exchange of the peace is also a bridge between the liturgy of the Word and the Holy Communion. It is not to be a "folksy" greeting of friends, a time to introduce ourselves to each other or to welcome a stranger, but a serious, solemn, liturgical action. We are exchanging God's gift of reconciling love with each other.. We greet one another as a peaceable people so that when we share the body and blood, the life and love of Christ, we might do so as a people who are truly one in Christ.

Regretfully, this symbolic act can be a farce. Vincent Donavan, a Roman Catholic missionary to the Masai in Africa, tells of the beginnings of new communities of baptized converts and how he helped them create culturally authentic rituals. The Masai had a natural way to make peace with each other. They would exchange grass. So when they got to the exchange of the peace in the liturgy, they would do just that. But what was unique was their appointment of one of their number to watch carefully and, if everyone did not exchange grass with everyone else, the mass was ended and there would be no communion until reconciliation had been made. Why? They knew that to act as if they were all reconciled when they were not would be to sin against the body. Having been granted the gift of God's forgiving, reconciling love, we are obliged to share it with those from whom we may be estranged.[5]

This does not imply that every person must exchange the peace with every person present. That could turn the exchange of the peace into a parish party with little theological significance. What it does mean is that the congregation takes seriously the establishment of reconciliation before communion. Personally, I would make one exception. If someone wants very badly to forgive another, but seems unable to do so, if he or she honestly brings this desire to communion hoping that the experience will enable him or her to do so, it would be appropriate to commune. Regretfully, there are those who come to communion who are estranged and have no desire to forgive. In so far as estranged people rarely sit next to each other, they are not confronted by their need to exchange God's peace.

The Eucharist gives us all an opportunity to reflect on our estrangements, to accept the gift of God's unmerited love, and then, in gratitude, to share it freely with those who need it. This forgiveness is not so much the creation of something new as it is the letting go of something old. To forgive is not to cheapen or forget the past, but it makes a new future possible. Forgiveness is about the future, because there is no way to ease or forget the past. We always carry the past with us into the future; the issue is how we carry it with us. Forgiveness means being liberated from the hurt of the past, hurt we have caused or received, so that we can move on. Nevertheless, while forgiving others is difficult, not doing so will hurt us more than the person who needs to be forgiven. In any case, it is not impossible, for with God all things are possible.

Holy Communion

What follows after the service of the Word is Holy Communion. We begin with an introductory comment and overview. The study of comparative religions reveals that there are many similarities in all religious rituals. First is the experience of a transcendent reality, a mysterious sacred presence of the divine. For Christians, this is what we mean by the real presence of Christ in consecrated bread and wine. Second is ritual sacrifice in which the meaning and purpose of human life and its relationship with the divine is dramatized. This is typically a relationship of absolute dependence on the divine for life and the acknowledgment of a need for unity with the divine that only the divine can make possible. For Christians, this is revealed in the making present again of Christ's sacrifice on the cross, which is intended to draw us back into union with God and make us aware of God's gracious act in granting us the gift of salvation, the experience of life's wholeness and health. And there are sacred meals that provide us with the experience of unity with the divine and the consequent reception of transformed life. As Christians, we experience this reality in the reception of Holy Communion.

Prepare the Table

The traditional name for this first action in the second part of the Eucharist, in Greek the *anaphora*, the offering, is the Great Thanksgiving. Within each of our eucharistic prayers is a line such as "and offering to you, from the gifts you have given us, this bread and this cup, we praise you and we bless you" (Eucharistic Prayer D). What we, therefore, are really doing at this point in the liturgy is only "collecting" that which we will offer later and preparing the table for that action. Laypersons representing the congregation bring to the altar table gifts of bread and wine, those gifts of God and the work of our human hands that will become our spiritual food and drink. The symbolism requires, I believe, real wine and not grape juice, real bread baked by members of the congregation and not wafers. We also bring monetary gifts as symbols of our labors and our very selves—in their brokenness and incompleteness, still sacrifices holy and acceptable to God. The symbol of this self-offering in our society is also monetary, which means that the symbolic meaning of the action can be missed. For many, this "offering" is a collection of money to support the operating budget of the parish rather than an offering of one's life and labors. The symbol of this self-offering is further distorted by the fact that many people, those who pledge and pay their pledge each month by check (or in some churches by automatic withdrawals or credit cards), put nothing in the offering plate on Sunday. And rarely do the choir, liturgical ministers, or clergy participate in this important symbolic action of placing a financial gift in an alms basin. Alms are gifts to support the poor and needy, and there was a time when all the loose offering (money not in a pledge envelop) went for outreach programs of the parish, the diocese, or the national church, as a sacrificial gift beyond the pledge. How easy it is to neglect important symbolic liturgical actions, in this case the sacrifice of our lives so that God might take our lives and transform them and give them back to us made whole, infused with the life of Christ, so that we might go forth to love and serve in his name. Just as the Holy Spirit will transform bread and wine into the presence of Christ and his unconditional, unmerited, unending, redeeming love, the Holy Spirit can transform our lives and make them whole and holy.

All of life, of course, is Eucharist, a movement of adoration and gratitude toward God, a movement in which the meaning and purpose of life is revealed and experienced. We bring food, that which is necessary for life, money, and ourselves, acknowledging that what we offer to God is that which God has first given to us.

Make Eucharist

Next comes the Great Thanksgiving. Taking a moment to digress, let us consider the title given to the bishop or deacon who prays this prayer, the celebrant. A better title, I believe, would be president, the one who presides at our altar-table. The whole community participates in this celebration. Together we are the celebrant. That symbolic truth is perhaps seen best in Eucharistic Prayer C. It is for this reason that I have difficulty with con-celebrations by more than one priest. The presiding priest's responsibility is to aid the community to act together in celebrating the communal meal. Too many clergy at the altar distort the symbol.

There are eight alternatives in our prayer book, two in Rite I, four in Rite II, and two outlines following "An Order for the Celebration of the Eucharist." Each has its own emphasis. For example, Rite II Prayer A is especially relevant for the seasons of Lent and Easter; B for the seasons of Advent, Christmas and Epiphany; C for the Sundays after Pentecost; and D for special occasions. Others have been authorized and more will emerge over time, but they all have common features.

The Great Thanksgiving begins with an opening dialogue or greeting between the presiding priest and people and in the giving of thanks, just as we might introduce grace before an ordinary meal. We are invited to "Lift up our hearts," and we accept. It is our invitation to focus our attention on being lifted up into the reign of God. We do not bring the ascended Christ down to be with us—we go to him and experience life in his kingdom. Then our dialogue continues with "Let us give thanks," let us make Eucharist together for all that God has done for our salvation and the salvation of the world.

Then comes a joyful thanksgiving known as the preface. This is a specific thanksgiving to God for his work in and his revelation to his people, varying according to an occasion or season of the church year. This thankful recalling of God's mighty acts is punctuated by a congregational acclamation of praise: "Holy, Holy, Holy" *(Sanctus)* and "Blessed is the name of the Lord" *(Benedictus)*. And then we continue to offer thanks for the redeeming work of Christ as recorded in scripture. That is, we praise God for the salvation of the world through Jesus Christ our Lord.

This is followed and culminated by the words of institution—the commemoration of the event in which Jesus instituted the Lord's Supper. "On the night before he died for us . . . Take and eat, this is my Body which is given for you, blood which is shed for the forgiveness of sins. . . ." We are reminded that Christ gave his life in order that we who by our actions have estranged ourselves from God might be drawn back into a new reconciled covenant relationship. In the Western church it was these words said by the priest that made us aware of Christ's presence in our midst. The custom was to perform some symbolic act to acknowledge that fact, but in our contemporary prayers, the Eastern church's emphasis on the work of the Holy Spirit has been incorporated; therefore, we wait to acknowledge Christ's presence until the end of the eucharistic prayer when everyone in the community performs some symbolic act. The words of institution end with "Do this in remembrance of me." The question is: Do what? And the answer is: Do what is necessary to become who you already are through your baptism, my body, my presence in the world, which is the purpose of our making Eucharist together.

And then we recount what Christ did, is doing, and will do that makes this possible. "Christ has died, Christ is risen, and Christ will come again." Past, present and future are all brought into the present in the same manner that the reign of God—has come, is coming, and will come in its fullness—is brought into the present for us to participate in and experience. To remember, therefore, is neither to repeat that which occurred in the past nor to recall what happened long ago. It is to make present again that which happened once long ago and that will occur in the future that has not yet become reality. This remembering *(anamnesis)* before God of what Jesus Christ has done is followed by the memorial of his sacrifice *(oblation)*.

Here we make our offering of bread and wine, money, and our lives. Next, we invoke the Holy Spirit *(epiclesis),* asking God to send the Holy Spirit upon these gifts and upon the congregation. That is, to sanctify, to make holy, the bread and wine to be Christ's presence among us, and for us to receive Christ's life into our lives, transforming them to be Christ's body, the church, in the world. Triumphantly and joyfully, all concludes with a Trinitarian doxology and Amen.

It is important that we do not forget the difference between magic and a sacrament. Magic is when we do something to make something happen that wouldn't occur without our action. Sacraments do not make something happen; rather, they make us aware of what has already happened. Now that is not insignificant, because we cannot appreciate or experience that of which we are unaware. The eucharistic prayer does not make Christ and his love present among us, it makes us aware of Christ's presence and love, which are always among us.

What follows is a eucharistic prayer I wrote for use in an innercity church, St. Luke's, Atlanta, during the season that follows Pentecost when we reflect upon the implication of God's story of salvation for our lives as the body of Christ:

> The Lord be with you
> *And also with you*
> Lift up your hearts
> *We lift them up to the Lord*
> Let us give thanks to the Lord our God
> *It is right and good to give God thanks and praise*

Father, with thankful hearts we acclaim you as creator of all that is visible and invisible, and we wonder at our creation in your image and likeness. We also express our deep sorrow for our continuing rebellion against you and your will, as well as our eternal gratitude for your never-ending grace and mercy. Therefore, we join our voices with your children in every time and place, who forever sing this hymn to proclaim your thanks and praise:

> *Holy, Holy, Holy Lord, God of power and might,*
> *Heaven and earth are full of your glory.*
> *Hosanna in the highest.*
> *Blessed is the one who comes in the name of the Lord.*
> *Hosanna in the highest.*

With this unending hymn ringing in our ears, we take great joy in knowing that you choose to share our humanity and thereby opened for us the possibility of new and unending life. We are brought to tears by your willingness to suffer and die that we might know how much you love us. And we will be always grateful that you have promised to be with us through your Holy Spirit.

And so we might be Christ's body, Christ's presence in the world bringing liberation to captives, forgiveness to sinners, healing to the sick, food to the hungry, shelter to the homeless, love to the loveless, security to the anxious, hope to the hopeless, solace to the poor, reconciliation to the estranged, and peace to the warring, you sent us Jesus to be our example.

We remember his concern and love for the city when he wept over Jerusalem, crying, "Jerusalem, Jerusalem, the city that kills the prophets and stones those who are sent to it. How often have I desired to gather your children together as a hen gathers her brood under her wings and you were not willing." We also remember the earlier words of the prophet Jeremiah, "Seek the welfare of the city . . . and pray to the Lord for its benefit, for in its welfare you will find your welfare." And we remember the vision shared with the early church by the author of the Revelation of John, "I saw a new heaven and a new earth . . . I saw the holy city, the new Jerusalem coming down out of heaven from God." And so we proclaim the mystery of faith:

Christ has died, Christ is risen, Christ will come again.

Now recalling that by our baptism we were made citizens of a heavenly city called to make our way through this earthly city—loving mercy, seeking justice, and humbly walking with you, our God—we find ourselves surrounded by a city's needs and problems. And so we come from far and wide into the city we love and to this holy place to make Eucharist and so be nurtured and nourished for faithful life and service in the city of Atlanta.

And, therefore, we remember how on the night in which Jesus gave himself up for us, he took bread, gave thanks, broke it, and gave it to his friends, and said, "Take, eat, this is my body which is given for you. Do this in remembrance of me."

When the supper was over, Jesus took the cup, gave thanks to you, and gave it to his friends and said, "Drink this, all of you; this is my blood of the new covenant, poured out for you and for many for the forgiveness of sins. Do this as often as you drink it in remembrance of me."

And so we offer you this bread and this wine, your gifts to us which we return to you, along with food for the hungry, monetary gifts as symbols of our labors, and our very own lives as a sacrifice of praise and thanksgiving.

Pour out your spirit on this ordinary bread and wine that it might become for us Christ's presence, Christ's life and love, so that as we commune together we might experience life in the reign of God and be empowered to abide in it throughout the coming week.

All this we ask through your son, Jesus Christ. By Christ and with Christ and in Christ, in the unity of the Holy Spirit, all honor and glory are yours, Almighty Father, now and forever. Amen.

We next pray together the prayer Jesus taught his disciples, which in this case is intended to focus on how we are to abide in the reign of God until it comes in its fullness. We are to make holy, that is, to manifest in our lives the character of God; we are to live for the coming of God's reign in its fullness; we are to know and to do God's will; we are to live as a reconciled and reconciling people, always totally dependent on God, because only with God's help, God's grace, God's presence among us, can we be Christ's body in the world.

The church is called to be a community of faith in which God's reconciling power is made conscious, known, living, and active, so that we as a community might be the body of Christ, God's reconciling presence in the world until God's reign has come in its fullness. The church is a gathering of those to whom the ultimate destiny of all life has been revealed, and having accepted that revelation, they pray for the grace to live accordingly.

Break the Bread

In the past, the priest would break the bread during the words of institution when he said, "Jesus took bread and when he had given thanks, he broke it, and gave it to his disciples. . . . " But this manual act obscures the real meaning of this symbolic action. As in the Emmaus story, the crucified and risen Christ is made known to us in the breaking of the bread, and we experience a new exodus, our passing over from death to life. The breaking of the bread is the most important action preparatory to the distribution of consecrated bread and wine. By eating from a single loaf broken and a common cup distributed to all, the table community that is the body of Christ is reunited and is made known. We need to maintain a few moments of silence to gaze upon this symbol and experience its mystery. And then, as the community sings of this mystery, the bread and wine can be prepared to be given to the people.

Share the Gifts of God

Communion follows the ancient invitation: "The gifts of God for the people of God." We, the friends of God and people of peace, come forward to receive "the Body of Christ, the bread of heaven" and "the Blood of Christ, the cup of salvation." It is the life and love of Christ that we are offered and take into our lives. We believe in Christ's "real presence" in consecrated bread and wine. But we have chosen not to describe how Christ is present (as Roman Catholics have done in their doctrine of transubstantiation).

Still, there are a number of unresolved issues to be addressed. We have already discussed open communion. A second issue has to do with intercommunion, especially between Roman Catholics and Episcopalians. Roman Catholics hold that communion is a meal of reality, the gathering of the one, holy, catholic, and apostolic church. It is a meal that celebrates the reality of a single united body of Christ. And since that reality is not yet realized, it would be inappropriate for us to receive communion in a Roman Catholic church. However, we hold that this is a meal of anticipation. That is, while we are not yet united, we believe that if all baptized Christians communed together, they would long for and commit themselves to doing what is necessary to become one. We, therefore, invite and welcome Roman Catholics to commune with us. These two positions are complimentary in that each speaks to one dimension of the truth. A third issue has to do with the communion of baptized infants who have not been confirmed. Today baptized babies are welcome to receive as soon as they demonstrate a desire to do so. This is difficult for some parents to understand. They remember the days when you could not receive until you were confirmed, but we need to understand that this earlier conviction was based on the importance of understanding the Eucharist before we commune. This conviction was based on the idea that we had to intellectually understand a reality before we could experience it. Now we know that we have to experience a reality before we can understand it. In any case, who fully understands this sacrament known as the great mystery?

One other detail in terms of symbolic actions needs to be mentioned. It is important that we do not grab or take the bread ourselves. We are to open our hands to be given it as a gift. This holy food is not something we deserve, nor is it something that we can give to others unless it has first been given to us. The same holds true for the wine. It is not appropriate for us to intinct (dip the bread into the wine ourselves) or take the chalice from the server to drink. The server is to dip the bread in the wine and place it on our tongue and to hold the chalice while we assist in bringing it to our lips. The Eucharist represents God's grace, and we must receive it as gift.

Go Forth to Love and Serve

When the feast is over, the people of God give thanks for the gift received and pray that they may bear its fruit. And then, so that we do not forget the relationship between our ritual life and our daily life and work, we are dismissed into the world for a life of mission and ministry. We are sent out "to do the work God has given us to do, to go forth in the name of Christ to love and serve, to rejoice in the power of the Holy Spirit."

We cannot stay in the nest, in the comfortable coziness of God's loving embrace. We need to return to the trials and temptations of daily life, where we will be challenged to love and serve Christ with singleness of heart.

What is most important is that we are united in our understandings. Our practices can be diverse. There will always be various local customs. For example, some use red and some churches use white wine, sherry or port; some use wafers and some bread. Some stand and some kneel for prayers and communion. In some churches, only the priest serves communion; in others, the priest and authorized lay eucharistic ministers do so. In some, the priest must serve the bread; in others, anyone can. Some believe you must receive at the altar rail (wrongly referred to as the communion rail), and some have stations at various places in the church. Some believe in saving and reserving consecrated bread and wine in a tabernacle behind the altar or in an ambry nearby so as to have it available for those who could not be at communion; some believe all the bread and wine should be consumed at the end of the liturgy. There will always be differing styles for liturgy. Some will be more formal and elaborate and others more informal and simple. Culture should play a part in informing how we celebrate and the music we use. Participating in this diversity can be exciting. But keeping to the structure we have described can unite us and make us at home at a Eucharist in another culture with a language we do not speak. Knowing where we are in the liturgy makes it possible for us to insert our own language, and the symbolic actions can unite us in a subliminal way.

As Anglicans/Episcopalians, we have historically tolerated a wide range of theological and moral convictions. We have been united by our worship. We are a prayer book people and gathering at the table to make Eucharist together unites us. May we never forsake this historic principle. Or perhaps better, may the church be a place where we gather to pray together so that our differences might be dissolved rather than a place we go to have our similarities confirmed and our differences condemned.

CHAPTER 8

LIVING AS A RECONCILED AND RECONCILING PEOPLE

The most pervasive and powerful of the gospel images for the mission of Jesus is the coming reign of God. And one of the dominant aspects of this image is reconciliation. The reign of God is finally manifested as the union and communion of all human beings with God and each other.

The forgiveness of sins is inseparable from this gospel image. Jesus' ministry focused on the forgiveness of sins and the reunion of the separated. Christ died out of love for sinners and his death was intended to bring about the reconciliation of those who are estranged. As St. Paul wrote to the church in Corinth, "All this is from God who through Christ reconciled us to himself and God gave us the ministry of reconciliation; that is, in Christ God was reconciling the world to himself and entrusting to us the ministry of reconciliation" (2 Corinthians 5:18–19).

As our catechism in the Book of Common Prayer 1979 puts it, "The mission of the church (that is, the baptized) is to restore all people to unity with God and each other in Christ" (p. 855). I would add to this mission the unity with one's true self, the self that is in the image of God, and nature or the rest of God's creation.

Historically, Baptism is the church's primary sacrament of reconciliation. Baptism is intended to provide us with an experience of forgiveness for our sins, that is, we are washed clean, reunited with God, and empowered to live a new life. And at our baptism, we promise "to persevere in resisting evil and whenever (not "if") we fall into sin repent and return to the Lord" (BCP, p. 304). And the Eucharist, sometimes referred to as our second baptism, is our continuing sacrament of reconciliation. Each week we experience the reconciling love of God and we are empowered to go forth and forgive as we have been forgiven, to love as we are loved. Our tradition also includes a prescribed daily confession of sin and a separate Rite of Reconciliation.

Protestants have only two sacraments: Baptism and Eucharist. Roman Catholics have seven sacraments, one of which is the sacrament of reconciliation. Anglicans have two great sacraments and five lesser sacraments, of which the Rite of Reconciliation is one.

It seems quite clear to me that we the baptized are to be a reconciled and reconciling people. And that implies the need to live a self-critical life, a life of self-examination, a life of confession and absolution.

In my experience, however, few people think of themselves as sinners. They acknowledge that there are sinners, but they are rarely among them. It is possible to conclude that this conviction is self-righteous arrogance, but I think it is more accurately a radical misunderstanding about both "sin" and "sins."

The concept "sin" refers to our character, that is, to our sense of identity and how we are disposed to behave. Sin has to do with our interior life, with the person we are becoming and with our experience of shame. The word "sin" refers to our external life, the behaviors or acts that we have performed, the person we are, and our experience of guilt.

Nursed anger is sin, a sin that if not addressed can lead to an act of violence against self or another, which is a sin. Since many of us only think in terms of behavioral sins, we might conclude that we are without sin.

To sin is to fail to be who, by God's grace, we really are, a reconciled, dependent child in the family of God. To sin is to behave in ways that estrange us from God, ourselves, others, and nature. Both are a matter of breaking and hurting relationships rather than of breaking laws.

There are other issues related to our misunderstandings about sins. A few examples follow. Too often we think only of acts of commission, things we have done that are wrong, and forget those acts of omission, things we have neglected to do that would have been right. Too often we think of our actions and neglect to consider our motives for these actions. We forget that we are not only to do that which is right, but to do it for the right reasons. It is right to act kindly to someone, but not if we do so to gain favor with that person. Too often we let the situation alone define the right or wrong of an action. We may be married and living in an abusive relationship. For the sake of our well-being, we may need to seek a divorce, but we still have broken our marriage covenant and therefore sinned. Too often we only think in terms of what is legal and not what is right, or we use the standard of how others act rather than some principle of right and wrong to judge our own actions. Too often we think in terms of how our behavior affects us and not how it may affect others. For example, I am late for an engagement and the traffic is heavy, so I drive up a turn lane and then cut back into the through lane so as to get an advantage over those who have lined up. Or we may sin when we choose a wrong value. Consider the fact that both freedom and equality are laudatory values. But what if they come into conflict? Which is the right value to choose? I would suggest that it must be equality, because God is biased toward those who do not have all they need and never will unless we give up some of our freedom to have all we desire.

Perhaps we can now understand why the forgiveness of sin and sins and reconciliation of sinners is so central to the Christian life of faith. It also should help us understand why we have a separate Rite of Reconciliation in our Prayer Book. And while all may, some should, and no one must participate in this sacrament (a typical Anglican point of view), it provides those who acknowledge that they are saints who sin and desire to live into their baptism a useful resource for their spiritual life and growth.

Regretfully, all too few Episcopalians participate regularly in this rite. Many of us have only seen Roman Catholics in the movies walking into a confessional, kneeling, and beginning their confession with "Bless me, Father, for I have sinned." Most of us are aware that Protestants do not have a Rite of Reconciliation. Therefore, I would like to address some of the misunderstandings and confusions that surround this rite and how to meaningfully participate in it so that we might live more faithfully as a reconciled and reconciling community of faith.

In the past, this ritual was referred to as either confession or penance. The word "confession" pointed to our need to acknowledge our sin and ask forgiveness for some action we performed that we believed to be sinful. The word "penance" pointed to a punishment we needed to accept if we were to be forgiven for some particular sin, that is, something we needed to do to make recompense for our sinful act. Both focused on what we were to do. The Rite of Reconciliation, on the other hand, points to what God has done and continues to do: God offers us forgiving love in order that we might be healed of our brokenness and incompleteness and returned to harmony with God, others, ourselves, and creation. The church is a community of forgiven and forgiving sinners who are living into their baptism by reflecting on their spiritual and moral lives and by doing what is necessary, with God's help and the church's support, to grown into ever-deepening and loving relationships. The Rite of Reconciliation provides us with a stimulant and resource to reflect on our lives as a baptized people in terms of broken relationships.

Our new rites of reconciliation reflect changing understandings of ethics. For a long time the study of ethics focused on moral decision making. Our focus was on behaviors, the breaking of laws, and the experience of guilt. We neglected to pay attention to the ethics of character. We focused on doing more than on being. Our conscience asks what we should do. Our character asks what kind of person we desire to become. Our conscience is concerned with doing God's will, while our character is concerned about how our behavior affects our relationship with God. Obviously, both are important. Conscience deals with our actions and character with our dispositions to act. When we focus our confessions on actions for which God forgives us and we are absolved, we may ignore the real sin that underlies our sinful action. For example, a person might confess to abusing a child. He or she might be truly remorseful and desire amendment of life, but after acknowledging God's forgiveness, he or she performs the same act again. The reason the person cannot put an end to the sinful behavior is that the person has not confessed the real sin, namely, the disposition that led to the sinful act.

Historically, certain things have been considered necessary for a faithful confession. We must understand the sacrament rightly. We do not participate in the rite in order to acquire God's forgiveness. God's forgiveness is not a reward for being remorseful or promising to change our behaviors. God's forgiveness is the source, and not the condition, of our regret and our desire to change our lives. It is because God's forgiveness is unmerited, unconditional, and unending that we are enabled to experience reconciliation and live a reconciled life.

It is important to remember that God does not give us what we deserve. God gives us what we need. God's judgment is not for retribution, but for reconciliation. We confess that Jesus died on the cross for our sins, but we often misunderstand this affirmation of faith. Jesus did not die on the cross to change the mind of God or to justify God's forgiving our sins. Jesus died on the cross to show us how much God loves us and how far God is willing to go to demonstrate his love and draw us back into his embrace. It is because God already loves us and forgives us that we are enabled to do that which is necessary to experience reconciliation with God.

The Rite of Reconciliation, therefore, is a sacramental action of the church that is intended to heighten our awareness and experience of reconciliation or reunion with God, our true selves, others, and God's creation. It is one of the ways the church lives out its mission to restore all people to unity with God and each other in Christ.

To participate in this sacrament faithfully, we need to consider the following: Have we named our sin rightly? For example, if someone comes to confession and confesses a sin that they have confessed before but have not repeated, he or she has not confessed the real sin. That sin is the inability to accept God's forgiveness. Further, if we center our confession on an action we have performed but have neglected to examine our values and attitudes, the motives and dispositions that led to that action, we may miss out on confessing our real sin.

Are we truly contrite and remorseful, and are we committed to make a firm resolve not to repeat the sin? This involves an honest admission of guilt or shame and not, for example, simply being sorry because we were caught or because we fear being punished. True contrition is being genuinely sorry for what we did because we know it was wrong and we intend never to repeat it again.

And we must be sincerely repentant. To repent is not simply to regret what we have done. It means that we are determined, with God's help, to change the direction of our lives. It implies a change of heart and will so that we might discern and do the will of God. The first step in the spiritual/moral life is to make sure we are traveling in the right direction. The evil one would have us aim for fame, fortune, and power (to be in control). Christ would have us aim for humility (to glory only in God), poverty (not to be attached to anything except God), and humiliation, acknowledging our weakness in controlling life and our lives (to be totally dependent on God).

Then, we need to be willing to make whatever restitution possible to any person or persons we have sinned against. And more importantly, we need to be committed to practice regularly whatever spiritual acts we believe will encourage and support our growth into an ever-deepening and loving relationship with God as well as improving how we are disposed to behave. For example, if the cause of a sinful behavior is the inability to love ourselves, we might adopt a daily practice of kneeling in front of the cross and looking up at Christ, who believes that we are lovable enough to die for. As we do so, we can meditate on our attitudes toward self love and the commandment "to love our neighbor as ourselves"—or better, to love ourselves and all others equally.

And last, we need to be willing to accept absolution or God's forgiveness, which implies our willingness to forgive those who have sinned against us and move on with our lives free from guilt and shame, empowered to live more faithfully as a baptized people.

While reconciliation is a major theme in both Baptism and Eucharist and is included within our daily life of prayer, the church has two specific rites for the reconciliation of a penitent (BCP, pp. 446–51). These rites take place in private in the presence of a priest. They offer us a unique opportunity to grow in our spiritual life. The reasons are multiple. First, typically we are not motivated to engage in the difficult and sometimes painful work of an honest confession unless we are accountable to another human being.

Second, the priest as a representative of the community can provide us with an awareness of both God's and the community's forgiveness, both of which we desire and need.

Third, if we are to name our sin faithfully and if we are to name a faithful penance, we need to discuss our confession with an insightful and spiritual person who is sworn to secrecy, someone with whom we can be absolutely honest.

We have two rites of reconciliation in our Prayer Book. I like to think of them as serving two different purposes. There are three types of guilt: natural guilt or shame, which deals with our interior life and our dispositions to sin; real guilt, which deals with our external life and sinful actions we have performed; and neurotic or misplaced guilt, such as blaming ourselves for something someone else has done or blaming ourselves for something someone else has done to us that requires pastoral counseling rather than confession.

Form I in our Prayer Book (p. 447) speaks more clearly to those struggling with natural guilt or shame and sorrow for sin and the person we are becoming by harboring particular dispositions to sin. This form, therefore, is best used in the context of spiritual direction and as an aspect of regular reflection on our spiritual and moral lives, our relationships with God, self, others, and nature.

Form I best serves our struggle to cope with natural guilt and can be used as a regular spiritual exercise. It begins with our request for a blessing. Reconciliation is hard work, and we cannot engage in it faithfully without God's help. The priest offers God's blessing on our intentions and thereby reminds us of God's grace or forgiving, reconciling presence. We then make our confession to both God and the church by making our confession in the presence of a priest

We then acknowledge responsibility for our sin and our desire to live a new life, with God's help and the church's support. Having made our confession, we ask for counsel, direction, and absolution. The priest, as symbol bearer of the church's faith and life, offers that counsel, and then announces absolution and offers us the kiss of peace, thereby sharing God's reconciling love. The priest ends the rite by sending us back into the world in peace with a request for our prayers, acknowledging that he or she is also a sinner.

Form II (p. 449) speaks to those suffering from real guilt. It is built upon images of the prodigal son or, perhaps better, on the compassionate father. It begins with our praying Psalm 51 with our confessor, followed by our request for prayer. The priest then announces the good news of God's forgiving, reconciling love, and we make our confession. When we finish, the confessor asks two questions. First, we are asked about our intentions and if we intend to lead a new life. Then, recalling the words from the Lord's Prayer ("forgive us our sins as we forgive those who sin against us"), the priest asks us if we are willing to forgive others as God forgives us. After we have answered both questions in the affirmative, the priest announces absolution and sends us forth in peace.

Let me explain the process in a little more detail, at least as I engage in it, especially with those who have never experienced a Rite of Reconciliation before. Anyone who wishes to participate in the Rite of Reconciliation calls and makes an appointment. For those who are engaging in this rite as part of their spiritual disciple once or twice a year (Lent is a traditional time), I recommend that they reflect on their lives since their last confession by comparing and contrasting their lives with the Ten Commandments, the Beatitudes in Luke's gospel, and the seven deadly sins.

While the Ten Commandments do provide a helpful guide for self-examination, many people have difficulty understanding their full

meaning. Therefore, I have paraphrased a dynamic equivalent transla-
tion of the commandments by Brian Haggerty as found in his book,
Out of the Slave House.[1]

1. Only God is worthy of unreserved faith and unbounded
trust. You therefore shall live for and serve only the one living
God.

2. You shall not advocate any religious, political, economic, or
social ideology or allow yourself to be committed to it.

3. You shall not lay exclusive claim to God's blessing for yourself or call upon God to bless you for selfish purposes.

4. You shall act reverently to the natural world and regard those
who labor with respect and dignity.

5. You shall treat all the elderly with deference and respect, for
they preserve the memory of the community.

6. You shall not threaten the lives of others by either aggressive
or irresponsible behavior.

7. You shall not threaten another person's marriage, committed
relationship, or family life.

8. You shall not deprive, in any way, another person's or group's
freedom.

9. You shall not permit any other person or group to be treated
unjustly.

10. You shall not grasp after what belongs to someone else or
seek for yourself that which belongs to all people.

The Beatitudes in the Gospel of Matthew (5:1–12) name the character traits or dispositions of those who comprise the body of Christ,
so this list may also be helpful in reviewing our lives in advance of the
Rite of Reconciliation. In Matthew's gospel, Jesus teaches his disciples
that God affirms:

1. The poor in spirit or those who live their lives totally dependent on God, putting their complete trust in God's grace.

2. Those who mourn or those who suffer deep sadness for both the sin in the world and their participation in it.

3. The meek or those who live between extremes of loving self too much or not enough.

4. Those who hunger and thirst after righteousness or those whose greatest desire is a right relationship with God and neighbor.

5. The merciful or those who live a life of forgiving, compassionate love.

6. The pure in heart or those whose motives are as pure as their actions.

7. The peacemakers or those whose life is dedicated to reconciliation.

8. And those who are willing to do God's will no matter the cost.

The classic seven deadly sins or better dispositions to sin can also be used to prepare for the Rite of Reconciliation. (Parenthetically, these sins were developed by and for men, therefore, women may experience their opposites; for example, in pride, men love themselves too much, but women often do not love themselves enough. I have combined the two extremes in my rendition of these seven dispositions to sin.

1. Pride: thinking too highly of one's self or thinking not highly enough of one's self.

2. Envy: wanting to be someone else or being who someone else wants you to be.

3. Anger: actually, nursed anger or the refusal to acknowledge anger.

4. Sloth: not caring or caring too much.

5. Avarice: the love of having things or wanting to have nothing.

6. Gluttony: eating and drinking more than is needed for health or maintaining an eating disorder.

7. Lust: treating a subject as an object or permitting oneself to be treated as an object.

Having prepared to participate in this Rite of Reconciliation, we are ready to do so. The Rite of Reconciliation can be conducted at the altar rail in the church, in a room set aside for the rite, or in a priest's office. I usually suggest that penitents go into the church and pray Psalm 51 before they come to see me. The appointment begins with some refreshments or some other act of hospitality followed by a prayer such as: "Reconciling God you are always more ready to forgive than we are to ask or accept your forgiveness, so it is in thanksgiving that we your children, saints who sin, come apart to make known your forgiving love and thereby grow in grace, and all for your love's sake."

We then have a conversation in preparation for the formal confession, discussing all the dimensions of a faithful confession, including appropriate penances. Then the penitent kneels and we participate in the sacrament as found in the Prayer Book together. After we have finished, I suggest the penitent return to the church and pray Psalm 103 before he or she leaves.

We humans were created in the image and likeness of God, that is, we are meant to live in unity with God, discerning and doing God's will. We were created as dependent children upon whom God chose to be dependent. We by nature can do nothing without God's help. God has chosen to do nothing without our help. Our relationship is one of interdependence and cooperation. We were created as communal beings to live together in God's reign of justice and peace. We were created with a free will so that we might live a cooperative relationship of love. In our freedom, we have a proclivity to want to be independent and manage life and our lives. We therefore experience estrangement and yet long for reconciliation. God, whose love for us is unmerited, unconditional, and unending, seeks after us with a forgiving spirit.

God's justice is tempered by mercy and God's judgment is for reconciliation, not retribution. We are called to be a reconciled people so that we might be a reconciling people. This sacramental Rite of Reconciliation in our Prayer Book is intended to aid us on our pilgrimage to grow in an ever-deepening and loving relationship with God and thereby with ourselves, all others, and God's creation.

CHAPTER 9
LIVING A LIFE OF WHOLENESS AND HEALTH

As we stated at the beginning of our last chapter, the most pervasive and powerful of the gospel images of Jesus' mission is the reign of God. We acknowledged that this image has numerous dimensions, and we named one of them "reconciliation." Now we will address another: salvation, whereby through the "inbreaking" of the reign of God into human history God restores persons and communities rent apart by demons of madness, disease, or whatever other dark forces lurk in the depths of the human heart waiting to destroy our humanity, tear us asunder, and deny our desire for wholeness and health.

Paul Lehman was a teacher of mine at Harvard in the late fifties. One of his memorable, lapidary phrases was, "The task of the church is making and keeping human life human." He was, of course, using the word human in two distinctive ways. "Human life" is the life of all those who are biologically classified as belonging to the species Homo sapiens. "Human" on the other hand, also refers to that which is really human, authentically human, fully human in the theological sense of God's intention for us. As the author of John's gospel records Jesus as saying, "I have come to bring you life in its fullness." Salvation is wholeness and health, wellness and well-being, the life of one who experiences fullness of life. And Jesus is our savior, the one who brings us salvation. As we profess in the Nicene Creed, ". . . for us and for our salvation, he (Jesus Christ) came down from heaven."

Dr. Lehman's phrase "keeping human life human" assumes that life in its fullness, while in one sense already realized, must be maintained. His phrase "making" assumes that life in its fullness is already in the process of becoming. For us Christians, Baptism both tells us what means to be fully human and makes us aware that we are made fully human by the action of God in Jesus Christ. But Baptism also marks the beginning of a process into that reality, that is, it sets us on a life-long pilgrimage of becoming who we already are.

To be fully human, to experience fullness of life, is to live in an ever-deepening and loving relationship with God. It is this relationship that makes possible healthy relationships with others. Our lives have meaning and purpose insofar as we strive to maintain this relationship with God. Because this is true, nothing and no one can destroy the meaning and purpose of our lives. This intimate unity with God is the only end for our lives. Everything else, including our closest human relationships, are to be means toward that end.

Perhaps, then, it would be better to speak of a "human becoming" rather than a "human being." And importantly, to speak of human becoming is to recognize that it is possible to become either more or less truly human. Which explains why we need the help and resources of the church if we are to experience wholeness and health.

The church teaches that we are made in the "image and likeness of God." This means that God has planted within us both the image of union with him and the drive to fulfill the potential of this reality. We humans do not have a soul. We are a soul, a soul that is a unified body, mind, and spirit, that can only know wholeness and health when living in community with other healthy souls.

The church began in a world where most believed that a human being was a body and a soul. The body was evil; the soul, good. When a person died, the body and soul separated and the soul lived on free from the confines of the body. This conviction was known as the "immortality of the soul." The church both adopted this understanding and advocated an alternative, namely, "the resurrection of the body." However, the immortality of the soul, with its negative attitude toward the body, especially in terms of sexuality and sex, has been detrimental and theologically questionable. A more theologically sound interpretation of Christian faith is the affirmation of the "resurrection of the body" combined with faith in the incarnation, that is, the conviction that this is God's good world and that God took on human form and entered this world; that is, God in Jesus took on our humanity as a unified and integrated body, mind, and spirit.

The roots of the words "holy" and "healthy" are the same. These roots point to wholeness, wellness, harmony, integration, and fullness of life. Following in the way of Jesus, the church has understood its ministry, its service to God, as being the "cure of souls." *Curare* is to care for or to look after. It is more than caring in the modern sense of feeling concerned about, or curing in the sense of eliminating a physical or mental/emotional malfunction. It is a concern for the human soul: a unified and integrated body, mind, spirit, a whole person, who has experienced God's purpose for human life, namely, the experience of living a life of wholeness and health. This is what the church means by being saved in both a material and nonmaterial, a this-worldly and an otherworldly, present and future sense.

This should help us understand why healing was at the very heart of Jesus' ministry. God's saving power over evil and the establishment of God's reign is primarily demonstrated in stories of healing. The disciples of Jesus were sent forth to share in this ministry. And the early church understood that healing was to play a major role in its life of witness to the gospel.

As the author of the Letter of James wrote: "Are any among you sick? They should call for the elders of the church and have them pray over them, anointing them with oil in the name of the Lord. The prayer of faith will save the sick . . ." (5:14ff.).

Over time, however, the church's understandings of salvation and healing changed. Salvation focused solely on the spiritual dimension of life and salvation became associated with life after death. The sacrament of the laying on of hands, the anointing of the sick, and practices of prayer—all understood as means to help people become aware of God's healing power and thereby to benefit from it—turned into acts of magic. That is, they became practices the church used to dispense God's healing power. Further, the church assumed that all physical and mental disease was caused by sin and the anointing of the sick became associated with the remission of sins just prior to death. It was this understanding that prevailed when "Extreme Unction" became one of the seven sacraments.

This understanding of the church's healing ministry had become so distorted and neglected that the Protestant reformers simply rejected it. With the death of the Age of Faith and the birth of the Age of Reason, modern science and medicine emerged as the sole means to deal with disease. While some Christians maintained a belief in spiritual healing, and Anglicans still considered anointing the sick and dying to be one of the five lesser sacraments, few took advantage of it.

One important exception to this rule was the Anglican priest and leader of the church's eighteenth-century evangelical revival, John Wesley. In his book *The Primitive Physick,* he talked about what we now know as holistic medicine. Wesley built hospitals and encouraged his parishioners to visit and pray with those suffering from disease. Wesley assumed there were various ways to deal with disease. With one ill person he prayed; with another, he applied a plaster. But prayer, according to Wesley, was always appropriate, for prayer always heals the person if not the malady. He also gave attention to prevention by counseling attention to diet (eat sparingly, be moderate in beer and wine, and eliminate coffee and tobacco), exercise (walk in the fresh air for two hours a day), rest (sleep eight hours each night), maintaining cleanliness, praying daily, and attending church regularly. He also formed small groups for spiritual formation and growth (including confession of sin and reconciliation) and for prayerful caring for each other's physical and mental health. Despite these pockets of interest in spiritual healing, by the twentieth century, few people saw the church as a resource for healing. We had a healing rite in our Book of Common Prayer, but it still connected disease with sin and focused on confession and absolution. Few took advantage of it. Some fringe groups in the church maintained a place for a healing ministry, but generally, the medical profession took the place of the church in dealing with disease.

Sadly, I must confess that while early in my ministry I prayed for and with the sick, I never expected my prayers to make any significant difference. Then, in the late sixties, I was sent as a delegate to a conference at the University of Paris. Organized by the Roman Catholic Church, it was entitled "Salvation: Wholeness and Health." As an aspect of the Vatican II Council's reforms that were sweeping the Roman Catholic Church, this conference was to reflect critically on the church's rites for the laying on of hands and the anointing of the sick.

A cultural anthropologist who had studied the relationship between religion and health in various cultures gave one of the lectures. He offered new definitions of words related to illness that were a revelation to me. Disease is a malfunction of the body or mind. A cure is the elimination of that malfunction. A sickness, on the other hand, is our attitude toward or response to a disease. Healing is a change in that attitude or response. The cure of disease might be the dominant concern of medical science, but healing was a spiritual matter. The human being is once again understood as a soul, a unified and integrated body, mind, and spirit in which each dimension affects the others. Sometimes a spiritual healing can contribute to a cure, sometimes not. But what the church promises is healing, healing that makes it possible to live fruitfully and faithfully, with or without the disease. Recall the example of St. Paul and his "thorn in the flesh," a disease that was never cured, but because he was healed, he was able to live faithfully and minister to others (2 Corinthians 12:7).

These new definitions and the light they shed on spiritual healing took on a human face with my post-conference visit to Lourdes, a place of pilgrimage for those suffering from disease in southern France. I arrived at Lourdes at night and I joined in a procession. Thousands of lit candles reminded us that Christ is the light of the world in the midst of the world's darkness. As we processed, some people carried icons of Mary and sang "Ave Maria." Along the pathway are springs that produce water out of the rocks. Pilgrims touched the water to their foreheads and crossed themselves, they washed their faces, and they drank. Every person was treated with dignity and respect. The most diseased went first. As they walked, they prayed the Rosary and murmured other prayers. Hands were laid on them and prayers were recited by laypersons, and they were anointed and blessed by a priest. While many amazing cures have occurred at Lourdes, I didn't witness any. No one threw away crutches or arose from a wheelchair. But not one face was left unchanged by the experience. Something had happened to them, and they would never be the same again. Neither would I. Their spirits had been healed, and that was truly a miracle.

I have witnessed the curing of diseases considered medically incurable through prayer, the laying on of hands, and anointing. But I have also witnessed those with a deep and abiding faith that have not been cured through these spiritual means. We need to be careful that we do not equate wholeness and health with the absence of physical or mental disease. After our resurrection, we believe that we will have a new body and mind that cannot suffer from disease. Ultimately, therefore, we are promised a cure as well as healing. Meanwhile, here on earth, if we are healed we can live a full, purposeful life, even though we continue to suffer with a physical or mental disease.

In scripture, Jesus tells many stories about healing, and some about curing. Throughout the gospels there are many stories that provide us with important spiritual insights about healing and curing.

- Luke's story of the ten lepers differentiates between healing and curing. All ten of the lepers were cured, but only one is healed, the one who returns to give thanks to God (Luke 17:12–19).

- In the story of the man with the skin disease (Matthew 8:1–4), we learn the significance of faith in healing. On seeing Jesus, the man says: "Lord, if you choose, you can make me clean." It was the man's own perception and awareness that we can be healed through the power of God's love that made him well.

- In the story of the paralyzed servant in pain (Matthew 8:5–13), we learn how the faith of others and their prayers can affect healing. The centurion goes to Jesus to seek healing for his servant, and it is the centurion's faith that prompts Jesus to heal. "And to the centurion Jesus said, 'Go; let it be done for you according to your faith.' And the servant was healed in that hour."

- The story of Peter's mother-in-law (Matthew 8:14–15) teaches the significance of touch, of the laying on of hands in healing. "When Jesus entered Peter's house, he saw his mother-in-law lying in bed with a fever; he touched her hand, and the fever left her." Touch can be important in the healing process.

- In the story of the possessed person (Matthew 8:28–34), we learn how the power of God's love can free our minds from those forces that keep us sick. Demons who inhabit two men are sent into swine instead, and the possessed men are freed.

- In the story of the paralytic (Matthew 9:1–8), we discover that sometimes our physical diseases are a result of guilt or shame and that forgiveness can make us whole. Upon entering a town, Jesus was approached by men carrying a paralyzed man on a bed. Surprisingly, Jesus makes a different response than we might expect. "When Jesus saw their faith, he said to the paralytic, 'Take heart, son; your sins are forgiven.'" In this case, Jesus saw what others did not, that in this case, forgiveness was the way to wholeness and health. But to convince them that the healing is complete, Jesus also instructs the paralyzed man to stand up and walk, which he does.

- And in the story of the woman with the hemorrhage (Matthew 9:18–26), we learn of the importance of desire if we are to be made well. As Jesus is walking in a crowd, "suddenly a woman who had been suffering from hemorrhages for twelve years came up behind him and touched the fringe of his cloak, for she said to herself, 'If I only touch his cloak, I will be made well.' Jesus turned, and seeing her he said, 'Take heart, daughter; your faith has made you well.'"

I am also sure that there were also those whom Jesus could neither cure nor heal. They exist in our own day. For example, sometimes our disease or sickness may have been diagnosed incorrectly. Sometimes we limit God's ability to cure us, refusing medical treatment, therapy, or prayer. Sometimes we counter God's desire for a cure by continuing behavior, such as smoking, that is the cause of the disease. Sometimes we continue to live a life estranged from God, or we have an unconscious desire to remain diseased or sick because we benefit from it and are unwilling to pay the price of a cure or healing. There are also times when we give up too soon, forgetting that healing is a long, slow, gradual process. Some people are unwilling to accept the help of others, believing they can get well on their own. Sometimes we continue to live in an unhealthy environment. Some pray only that their disease will be cured and not because they desire to live in an ever-deepening and loving relationship with God.

One thing is clear. God's will for us is always for wholeness, health, and healing. No one suffers from a disease as God's punishment for sin. We may suffer from a disease as a natural consequence of our actions, but it is never God's desire or will. Sin may contribute to a disease, but it is not the primary or most frequent cause. Cancer and schizophrenia are not God's will. They are the body at war with itself, cells or mental functions horribly disordered. No disease is given us as a "cross to bear."

To take up our cross is to be willing to do God's will regardless of the cost. No child dies of a disease because God wants to "bring the child home." A child dies because something went wrong. We do not know why God permits these malfunctions of our bodies and minds. But we do know that God will not abandon us. God is always present with us in our pain and suffering, seeking to provide healing and thereby redeem our maladies, turning negatives into positives, and granting us new life.

Today the medical profession is becoming aware of the value of holistic medicine that includes the spiritual dimension of human life. And clergy are being influenced by new understandings of spiritual healing. Increasingly, individuals with a physical or mental malady are turning to the church for spiritual healing. Many churches offer healing stations at the Sunday Eucharist at which a healing team of clergy and laity lay hands upon, pray with, and anoint those who suffer from some malady before they come forward to commune. Other churches have periodic healing liturgies.

Cures and healing take place through many means. Physicians and health professionals apply their knowledge and skills to cure us. The prayers and intercessions of individuals and communities help to create a connectedness between God and the person in need of healing. There are those who have charismatic gifts. By laying their hands on another, they create an environment in which God's energy can flow. Our own prayers place us in a relationship with God and open us to God's healing actions. And there are sacramental acts such as anointing that are intended to make us aware of God's healing presence and action so that we might benefit from it. Notice the words for the anointing of those with a malady: "I lay my hands upon you and anoint you in the name of our Lord and Savior Jesus Christ beseeching him to uphold you and fill you with his grace that you might know the healing power of his love" (BCP, p. 456). We also recognize that we can ask the Holy Spirit to empower us be an instrument of God's healing power in the life of another. The words that are used when someone comes to the church for another person's healing are: "May God empower you by the might of his Holy Spirit to be a healing presence in the life of N."[1]

Increasingly, congregations hold regular healing services using the "Public Service of Healing" in our *Book of Occasional Services,* which is an addendum to the Book of Common Prayer. In that liturgy, prayers are prayed for the sick, the injured, and the disabled that they may be made whole; for the lonely, anxious, and despondent that they may be made aware of God's presence; for those experiencing broken relationships that they may be healed; for those living with emotional distress that they may receive soundness of mind and serenity of spirit; and for the dying that they may be granted peace and a holy death (*Book of Occasional Services,* pp. 147–54).

For other insights about prayer and spiritual healing, we need to look at the collects for healing in the Book of Common Prayer (pp. 458–61).We are counseled to pray for people that they might be relieved of their sickness, comforted in their sickness, restored to health, returned to usefulness in the world, strengthened in their weakness, given confidence in God's loving care, that their illness may be sanctified, that they may gratefully accept the healing offered, and that they may know the healing power of God's love. Such prayers are God's will and, if prayed sincerely, will be answered. We need to remember that our prayers do not convince God to do something. They rather give God permission to do that which God already desires to do.

Healing is a charism of the church. As a baptized people, we are called to be a community of wholeness and health. It is not just a ministry of a few. It is a way of life lived by all who have been baptized into the body of Christ. Of course, there are those whose work is to help us to be such a community of faith. We now have directors of health ministry or parish health coordinators. These are men and women with training in nursing, public health, spiritual theology, or pastoral care. They teach about wholeness and health, they act as referral agents for any and all health needs, they train persons for specific health ministries, they organize and lead support and grief groups, and they coordinate volunteers and parish health committees. And they work as holistic health advocates.

A growing number of physicians and health care professionals also practice holistic medicine by treating the whole person in terms of the physical, mental/emotional, and spiritual dimensions of life. They understand wholeness and health, salvation, if you will, as something we are always moving toward, not something we possess. They recognize that in this journey toward wholeness and health there will be stress and many crises, harmony will be disrupted, and equilibrium will need to be reestablished. And the church has a role to play in this process.

Further, they know that no one should be defined by their uncured disease or labeled "handicapped." One who lives with diabetes or multiple sclerosis can be a whole and healthy person. I close this chapter with testimony by a parishioner on what it means to live into wholeness and health, to be saved.

Ken is forty and confined to a wheelchair. He was born with diabetes and spina bifida. He was given no hope for recovery. Nevertheless, he would tell you that he is a human being, a devout Christian with a disability, who thanks God every day for a fulfilled life. He explains that his disability has kept him close to God, God who has granted him wholeness and health. He remains paralyzed but still can serve God in every moment of every day. Ken is a member of our parish healing team who every Sunday can be found at our healing station. He gives thanks for the life and being of those who come for healing. He offers to God their lives in their brokenness and incompleteness. He images God's redeeming, transforming, healing love embracing them and giving them back their lives made whole so that they may go forth to love and serve in Christ's name. He explains that he knows the healing power of God's love and has been blessed with the charisma to help others know that love. And he confesses that it is the Eucharist that nourishes him and sustains him as he continues to grow in his relationship with God, which he believes is the meaning and purpose of his life. He has been saved, made whole and holy. Thanks be to God.

CHAPTER 10
LIVING A HOLY LIFE AND DEATH

From a philosophical perspective, death belongs to the finitude of human existence. Just as history must have a beginning and an end, so must every human life and history. If it were not so, history and life would have no meaning. True as this might be, it is hardly comforting.

Jeremy Taylor, a seventeenth-century Caroline Divine, was among the most influential voices during the formative period of the Anglican Church. During his short life of forty-four years, he buried two wives, his benefactors, and all of his seven children. Toward the end of his life, he wrote two books of practical advice for which he is most famous, *Holy Living* and *Holy Dying*.

He begins Holy Dying with a simple contention that "we are born to die." Aging begins at birth and we have no right to expect to grow to a ripe old age. We may not like to think of death; life is always too short. But referring to Ecclesiastes, he reminds us that nothing is lasting and everything we might seek (fame, fortune, power, knowledge, happiness) is vanity. Every single one of us will die, and dying well, according to Taylor, is a great spiritual art. It is an art to learn while we are alive and healthy. The best way to live life to the fullest is to spend it preparing for death, our own and those we love, for when death comes near we may have no time for preparations.

These views may seem morbid, especially for those of us who live in the United States in the twenty-first century. Due to the success of modern medicine, we live longer today than the people of Taylor's time did. Now we struggle with the moral question of when we should permit someone to die a natural death versus sustaining life with our modern technologies. We also live in a culture that does its best to deny the reality of death. But Taylor, as a Christian theologian, knew that birth and death are always related. Just as our birth is the beginning of our dying, so also our death is the beginning of our being born again. And for that reason, it is incumbent on us to prepare for a holy death.

Living a holy life, according to Taylor, requires that we devote our lives to the right end, namely, to grow into an ever-deepening and loving relationship with God. We must also live for others, all others, including those who will be born long after we have died. Another way to put it is that we must live a righteous life, a life committed to a right relationship with God, self, all others, and the natural world. As such, our lives should be devoted to the love of God and charity to all people. This way of life is founded on the practice of a variety of virtues, such as humility, forgiveness, moderation, generosity, gratitude, contentment, and patience. Further, we need to anticipate suffering and always remember that God suffers with us. So it is that suffering love is at the heart of life. At the same time, we need to acknowledge the presence of evil, but deny that it is from God.

We need to have few expectations and limit our desires. We need to understand that sickness and death are not from God. God's will is for wholeness and health, for fullness of life, and life with God forever. Taylor advises us to pray daily, to fast weekly, to keep the Sabbath, to worship regularly in the church each Sunday and on all holy days, to study and meditate on scripture, to tithe and give alms, to make a regular confession and seek spiritual guidance, and to use our time wisely in discerning and doing the will of God. Personally, I find his advice relevant to our own day.

However, living such a life is problematic. We have been raised in a society that is convinced that there must be a cure for every disease. We dream about, long for, and are dedicated to finding such a cure. Therefore, when faced with a disease for which there is no known cure, our faith is tested if not shattered. Nevertheless, in spite of all our knowledge and skill, we and all our friends and loved ones will die, many before we believe they should. We know this, and yet we still ask, "Why?" and "Where is God?"

It is often difficult for us to maintain our Prayer Book's faith in the resurrection. God did not create us because God was lonely and wanted our love. God created us because God needed to be able to share God's love, an unconditional, unmerited, and unending love, with his creatures. God is love and we are the subject of God's love. God's greatest desire is for us to be united in love. Because that is so, God had to create us with the freedom to reject God's love.

Further, God has an active and a permissive will. God does not will evil, sin, and death, but God permits them for a greater good. And that good is founded in God's desire and hope that we will choose to live with God in an ever-deepening relationship of love, a relationship that will last for eternity.

There are a host of understandings about what comes after death. For some, the answer is that nothing follows death; for others, we die but we live on in our good deeds and in the lives of our children; for still others, when we die we need to be prepared to go on a journey to find a resting place and therefore need to be embalmed and provided with food and other resources for the journey. And there are those who believe that we humans have a body and a soul, and that when we die only the body dies but the soul lives on. There are also those who believe in reincarnation, that is, that we will keep being reborn until, through our good works, we reach a state of nothingness. There are those who believe that our souls, separated from our bodies, live on in a sleep-like state until the end of time, when they will be reunited with their bodies. Obviously, those who hold this belief are opposed to cremation. Others believe that the soul goes to one of two places at death— heaven or hell—to be rewarded or punished for their life of faith or unfaith. For some, purgatory is a state in which we are given the opportunity to pay the price for our sins and to work out our salvation.

While Christians have held many of these positions, the traditional teaching of the church focuses on the resurrection of the body. It is an affirmation of faith founded on an amazing conviction, namely, that the human soul, understood as a material body, mind, and spirit, is destined to die, but has the capacity to be reborn with a new, nonmaterial body, mind, and spirit.

We are also confronted by a number of different images of heaven and hell. The one closest to our Prayer Book's understanding is that heaven is a state of being that we can experience both now and after our death. While our descriptions of this state are metaphorical, they all point to the experience of being one with God, which is the meaning and purpose of our lives. It is a condition that is never static and is both personal and communal. Further, it is a gift that cannot be earned, but one offered freely to all who will accept it.

Hell is also a state of being that can be experienced both now and after our death. It is the experience of being estranged from God and from other people. Hell is a consequence of our own choices and not a punishment from God. God wills no one to hell. Rather, God will never give up on anyone and will always do all God can do through love to draw each person back into God's embrace.

The church has always seen a foreshadowing of our end in our baptismal beginning. Baptism is our tomb, but it is also our womb. At our baptism, we experienced dying to sin, our separation from God, and God's love. Immersed in baptismal water, we were drowned. We lost our breath and experienced death. There was nothing we could do to save our lives. We have to let go of life and our desire to control and manage life so that God can breath new life, real life with God forever, into us.

At our baptism, the community of the baptized prays: "Thank you Father for the water of Baptism. In it we were buried with Christ in his death. By it we share in his resurrection. Through it we are reborn by the Holy Spirit." In Baptism, we have a foretaste of dying to all that enslaves us, dying to our old selves that we may be reborn. The reformer Martin Luther spoke of baptism as a dress rehearsal for death.

Part of us must die each day, he said, so that God brings us to new life. When asked if he feared death, Luther commented that he did not, because he had already died a hundred deaths beginning with his baptism, and each had led to new life. Our Christian hope at death is the same hope that sustains us throughout life, namely, that the God who has claimed us and loved us and held us in life will continue to do so in death. We believe this not because we believe in eternal life, but because we believe in the eternal love of God. We expect death from the beginning. Death is no surprise. It is that for which we spend our lives experiencing and preparing. Early Christians often referred to death as a "heavenly birthday," because on that day—that birthday— a Christian dies and is reborn into eternal life with God. Therefore, the white vestments they wore and the songs of joy they sang at their burials offered a distinct contrast to the somber, joyless practices of others.

However, during the Middle Ages, Christian funeral practices moved their focus from joy to fear. The church became preoccupied with hell, judgment, and purgatory. Death was understood as a final accounting, a prelude to the Last Judgment. The churches of the Reformation, while protesting against the mournful character of these medieval funerals and their preoccupation with the status of the dead person's soul, failed to restore the earlier focus on hope and comfort.

But all this has changed. Our Prayer Books' burial services today are held in the context of an Easter Eucharist (pp. 491–505). The paschal candle, the resurrection music, and the sacramental meal in the reign of God proclaim and show God's love amidst death and commend the deceased to God's gracious mercy and peace.

Eulogies are less common, because we have faith that, as in life, God's grace and love are our hope in death, not our good lives or our good deeds. Our trust and hope are not based on what we have done but upon our lifelong, daily experience of what God has done and is doing to make the experience of life, true and abundant life, possible now and forever. We do not believe in the noble pagan belief in the immortality of the soul. Immortality is not a human characteristic, an aspect of human nature. Eternal life is not a human achievement or an innate human possession. It is a surprising and graceful gift of a loving God who loves us in life and in death. Thus, resurrection is God's mighty act—and to it we witness.

Earlier we referred to a holy death. But finally, that is not the real issue faced by those of us who believe in the resurrection of the dead. The real issue is how to live a holy life, a new life, way of life made possible by our faith in the resurrection in the present as a testimony to our faith in Jesus' resurrection.

There is no greater event in history than the faith of a small group of men and women in the resurrection of the historical Jesus. It turned the Jesus of history into the Christ of faith. And it both transformed those who had experienced this resurrection into a community of faith and sent them forth into a hostile world to risk and lose their lives on behalf of this strange experience. Amazingly, their proclamation of Christ's resurrection caught the imagination of the masses and became the distinguishing mark of a new religion, Christianity. On every Sunday, the first day of the week, these Christians gathered to celebrate the death and resurrection of the Messiah, the Christ, the anointed one who had ushered in the long-desired and hoped for reign of God. Mysteriously, God, through the death of Jesus, had destroyed the power of evil and redeemed the world. Life— true, abundant, and eternal life—was now the reality that ruled. Through Baptism, the experience of death and resurrection, persons were initiated into this new reality and empowered to live accordingly, that is, to abide in God's reign until it came in its fullness.

I firmly believe in the resurrection of Jesus from the dead. But if you were to ask me why, I am not sure I could offer a reasonable and satisfactory answer. What I can say is that while I have been confronted by doubt and despair, ugliness and evil, hatred and estrangement, violence and destructiveness, suffering and death, I have also experienced faith and hope, beauty and goodness, love and reconciliation, wholeness and health. I have no words to describe it, but in the midst of death, I have known life and more than life. I have experienced the transformation of one negative after another in my life into an unexpected or unexplained positive. For this reason, I have no difficulty confessing with the church my belief in the resurrection and life after death.

There is a creative, nurturing, and redemptive reality that overarches our lives, relieves our anxiety, and provides us with hope and the stimulus to live a holy life in the face of death. That brings me back to my chapter on living into our baptism. God has made possible a new way of life for individuals and communities. In the mystery of death and rebirth, God has, through the life, death, and resurrection of Jesus, ushered in God's reign of justice and peace. Life in a domination-free, nonviolent, reconciled world, in which every human being receives all that he or she needs but no more, is as possible as life with God forever after death.

God has made possible a new way of life for individuals and communities. We can abide in God's reign now and forever. We can live, with God's help, a holy life, and by so doing, prepare for a holy death and rebirth to new life. And that is finally what it means to live as a prayer book people.

AFTERWORD

This is not intended to be an authoritative text on the Book of Common Prayer 1979. Rather, it is my personal attempt to share with laypersons and clergy, new and lifelong Episcopalians, how our 1979 Prayer Book has stimulated and informed my thinking about the Christian life of faith. Perhaps this volume is best understood as a reflective walk through our Prayer Book in which I share personal theological and liturgical reflections intended to stimulate conversation and further study among those of us who desire to be Anglican/Episcopal Christians at the beginning of the twenty-first century.

There are many fine theological commentaries on the Book of Common Prayer 1979, such as Leonel Mitchell's *Praying Shapes Believing* (Harrisburg, PA: Morehouse Publishing, 1985), and historical commentaries such as Marion Hatchett's *Commentary on the American Prayer Book* (New York: Seabury Press, 1980). There are fine historical and theological studies on particular services in our Prayer Book, such as Byron Stuhlman's *Occasions of Grace* (New York: Church Hymnal Corporation, 1995). There are significant works on the history of our Prayer Book, such as William Sydner's *The Real Prayer Book* (Wilton CT: Morehouse-Barlow, 1978) and Jeffrey Lee's *Opening the Prayer Book* (Cambridge, MA: Cowley, 1999). And there are numerous commentaries on the rubrics for our Prayer book such as Dennis Michno's *A Priest's Handbook* (Harrisburg PA: Morehouse Publishing, 1983) and Byron Stulman's *Prayer Book Rubrics Expanded* (New York: Church

Hymnal Corporation, 1987). I encourage you to read and reflect on these other important works on our Prayer Book.

Other books of John Westerhoff on issues related to our Prayer Book and published by Morehouse Publishing include the following:

A People Called Episcopalians
This small book intended for inquirers can be helpful to new and long-time Episcopalians. It includes chapters on Anglican Identity, Anglican Authority, Anglican Spirituality, Anglican Temperament, and Anglican Polity.

Holy Baptism: A Guide for Parents and Godparents
This small book is intended to be a resource for preparing parents and godparents for the baptism of a child. But sections of it can be useful for working with adults who are preparing to be baptized and for all baptized persons preparing for Confirmation or the renewal of their baptismal vows and covenant.

To Love and To Cherish: The Celebration and Blessing of a Marriage
This small book is intended to address the canonical requirements for marriage preparation and therefore focuses on theological issues related to marriage rather than personal or psychological concerns. As such, it can also be useful for those married couples who are considering celebrating an anniversary of their marriage as found in *The Book of Occasional Services*.

Grateful and Generous Hearts
This small book is on stewardship. This personal, moving testimony to good stewardship is a best seller in the United States and Canada. Many congregations have bought copies to send out to all their members.

Will Our Children Have Faith?
This is a revised and expanded edition of a classic. It is a substantial work that continues to inspire parents and congregations in the nurture of children, youth, and adults in the Christian life of faith.

NOTES

Chapter 1

1. See John Westerhoff, *A People Called Episcopalians* (Harrisburg PA: Morehouse Publishing, 2003).

2. Evelyn Underhill, *Worship* (New York: Harper, 1936).

3. Willard Sperry, *Reality in Worship* (New York: Macmillan, 1925), 163, 165, 168.

4. John Westerhoff, "Celebrating and Living the Eucharist: A Cultural Analysis," in *Alternative Futures for Worship: Eucharist,* ed. Bernard Lee (Collegeville MN: Liturgical Press, 1997).

5. Bruce Reed, *Dynamics of Religion* (London: Darton, Longman, & Todd, 1978).

6. Amos Wilder, *Theopoetic* (Philadelphia: Fortress, 1976).

Chapter 3

1. John Dominic Crossan, *The Dark Interval: Toward a Theology of Story* (Niles, IL: Argus, 1975).

2. Walker Percy, *Message in the Bottle* (New York: Farrar, Straus, Giroux, 1975), 119–49.

Chapter 5

1. Walter Brueggeman, *The Message of the Psalms* (Minneapolis, MN: Augsburg, 1984).

Chapter 7

1. James Farwell, "Baptism, Eucharist, and the Hospitality of Jesus," *Anglican Theological Review* 81 (2004): 215–38.

2. David Steinmetz, "The Superiority of Pre-Critical Exegesis," *Theology Today* 37 (1980): 27–38.

3. Richard Hooker, *Of The Laws of Ecclesiastical Polity,* vol. 1., ed. John Keble (Ellicott City, MD: Via Media, 1994).

4. R. Taylor Scott, " Preaching: Rhapsodic, Rhetorical, and Liturgical," *College of Preachers Newsletter* 30 (Winter 1985): 1–3.

5. Vincent Donavan, *Christianity Rediscovered* (Notre Dame, IN: Fides/Claretan, 1978).

Chapter 9

1. Byron Stuhlman, *Prayer Book Rubrics Expanded* (New York: Church Hymnal Corporation, 1987), 167.

ABOUT THE AUTHOR

The Rev. & Dr. John H. Westerhoff, an Episcopal priest, studied theology at Harvard University and the historical and philosophical foundations of education at Columbia University. For twenty years he was professor of theology and Christian nurture at Duke University and priest associate at the Chapel of the Cross in Chapel Hill, North Carolina. International lecturer and author of numerous books, including the classic *Will Our Children Have Faith?*, he has for the last decade been theologian-in-residence at St. Luke's Episcopal Church in Atlanta, Georgia. Most recently he has been Visiting Professor of Anglican Studies at The General Theological Seminary in New York.

Also by
JOHN H. WESTERHOFF

A People Called Episcopalians: A Brief Introduction to
Our Peculiar Way of Life

Holy Baptism: A Guide for Parents and Godparents

Grateful and Generous Hearts

To Love and To Cherish Until Death Do Us Part:
Preparing for the Celebration and Blessing of a Marriage

Morehouse books are available through Episcopal bookstores,
or directly from the publisher at 800-877-0012 or
online at www.morehousegroup.com.

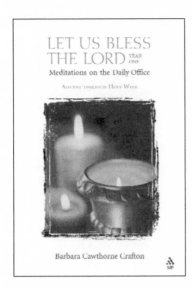

Let Us Bless the Lord, Year One: Advent through Holy Week

Meditations on the Daily Office

Barbara Cawthorne Crafton

Popular author, retreat leader, and priest Barbara Crafton communicates with thousands of subscribers to her daily e-mail meditations. They—and others who say the Daily Offices—will treasure this collection of brief meditations. Based on the assigned biblical texts for each day of the Church year, Crafton's writings complement perfectly the morning, noon, evening, and nighttime prayers that are the Daily Offices.

Crafton brings her trademark humor, pathos, and marvelous storytelling ability to *Let Us Bless the Lord*, as she shows contemporary readers how texts written centuries ago still speak clearly to us today. This is the first of four volumes that provide meditations for the entire Daily Office cycle.

Morehouse books are available through bookstores, from online booksellers, or directly from the publisher at 800-877-0012 or online at www.morehousegroup.com.